No Time Off
for good behaviour

D1211830

H.E. Woolley

GSPH

Published by

GENERAL STORE
PUBLISHING HOUSE INC.

1 Main Street, Burnstown, Ontario, Canada K0J 1G0
Telephone (613)432-7697 Fax (613)432-7184

ISBN 0-919431-33-X
Printed and bound in Canada.

Designed by Hugh Malcolm, Marlene McRoberts and Bill Slavin

Copyright ©1990
The General Store Publishing House Inc.
Burnstown, Ontario, Canada

General Store Publishing House Inc. gratefully acknowledges the
assistance of the Ontario Arts Council.

Canadian Cataloguing in Publication Data

Woolley, Ted, 1921-1990
  No time off for good behavior

ISBN 0-919431-33-X

  1. Woolley, Ted, 1921-1990. 2. World War,
1939-1945--Prisoners and prisons, German. 3.
World War, 1939-1945--Personal narratives,
Canadian. 4. Prisoners of war--Canada--Biography.
I. Title.

D811.W66A3 1990   940.54'7243'092   C90-090295-7

First Printing September 1990

Dedicated to the Memory of

Warrant Officer Robert Woolley, RCAF,
killed on operations over Nüremberg on February 23, 1943,
and whom I never saw in uniform,

Sergeant Jeffrey Reid, RAF,
killed by a German guard at Stalag VIIIB while attempting to
remove boards from a fence for firewood in January 1942, and

Sergeant Teddy Joyce, RAF,
machine-gunned at the wire at Stalag Luft III in July 1942
while attempting to escape by cutting his way through.

Acknowledgements

Grateful thanks are due to several people who helped in preparing this book for publication.

I am indebted to John Metcalfe for his advice and assistance in the preliminary editing of the manuscript.

To my wife Wynne goes a sincere thank-you for the patient reading of first drafts, and her valuable suggestions.

To Marjorie Czuboka who translated pages of hand-written manuscript to excellently typed material through first and second drafts.

To Bill Czuboka whose knowledge of the intricacies of word processing proved invaluable in producing copy acceptable to the publisher.

To Ray Silver, editor of *The Camp*, who gave kind permission to reproduce photographs used in this book I also offer my thanks.

To General Store Publishing House Inc. for their demonstrated faith in the work, and particularly to Marie Baird for her invaluable editing of the final text.

Table of Contents

Sergeant Pilot Ted Woolley, showing off newly won wings just before proceeding overseas in January 1941.

Introduction

The subject of prisoner-of-war escape and adventure has been covered many times in the past by other writers. *The Wooden Horse* and *The Great Escape* are classics of suspense, and hold the reader's undivided attention as the drama unfolds. Both of these stories were quite faithfully made into gripping films which even today are viewed by a new generation of watchers of the late, late show.

My purpose in writing these stories has been to make the important point that prisoner-of-war existence had another aspect. It was not all do or die, cloak-and-dagger matching of wits with our captors. That is not to say that I did not pay my dues. I tunnelled with the best of them and had my fair share of tunneller's elbow (which is a close relative of housemaid's knee). I have had the horrifying experience of being in a tunnel which collapsed; I was dragged almost hysterical to the cooler, there to repent our foolhardiness in digging in sandy soil without sufficient cross-bracing. To this day I feel uncomfortable in underground structures of any sort.

But there is another aspect which I should like to emphasize. Some of it was damnably funny - even hilarious! After all, we were young, generally in good health and spirits, and full of optimism, in spite of our occasionally degrading conditions. Bernard Shaw was once quoted as saying that "Youth is wasted on the young." Had he ever been subjected to life in a

German prison camp, he would have realized that the biggest thing we had going for us was our youth and its accompanying natural resiliency, and our ability to find humour in almost any situation.

For example, many of the "Dear John" letters received by prisoners of war might be considered almost tragic for the hapless men whose sweethearts had given up waiting for them. But no! Consider the forlorn and deserted lover consenting to have the fact made public by posting, on the camp bulletin board, an extract from his girl friend's letter stating that she had just had a baby. The unlucky recipient had been "in the bag" nearly two years!

These stories are not fiction. All of them are drawn from my recollections of three and one-half years in captivity. Naturally the conversations have been reconstructed, but the basic facts are unchanged, reinforcing my unavoidable conclusion that no situation was without its humorous side.

The ability of the average British soldier, sailor or airman to rise to any given occasion is not to be challenged. Add to this the fact that our camps were composed mostly of Englishmen, liberally sprinkled with a Cockney element (whose sense of humour is legend), and it becomes not at all surprising that many potentially disagreeable situations became the stuff of which high farce is made. We had working in our favour that inherent capacity of the mind which blots out unpleasantness by declining to accept that circumstances are as bad as they appear. We refused to take the situation as seriously as our captors.

Man, as distinct from other beasts, is the only animal capable of laughter. In fact he has been called the laughing animal. He laughs at wit which is very often malicious; he is amused by satire which is usually unkind. Comedy itself has at its very root the misfortunes of others, and is therefore different from humour which is sympathetic, playful, and very rarely destructive. But most of all man laughs at himself. It is this exclusive ability to find humour in his own misfortune which I hope to affirm. It may be that the humour contained in these anecdotes may be more obvious to ex-prisoners of war, and therefore might be somewhat obscure to those who did not experience the events firsthand. If I am guilty of trying to pass off inside jokes on unsuspecting readers I apologize and take refuge in the excuse that, as prisoners of war, we developed a somewhat warped sense of humour which will probably remain with us forever.

Some of these stories are very definitely not funny or amusing. Just as comic relief sometimes provides a counterpoint to high drama or tragedy, these stories have been included to help make my point: there is humour to be found in almost any situation if one looks hard enough.

I should like to acknowledge the book of sketches and cartoons entitled *Handle with Care* published in 1946 by two ex-prisoners, R. Anderson and D. Westmacott. I drew some of the inspiration for these stories from the humorous drawings which these gentlemen created during their years of captivity. Since their book dealt mainly with some of the more whimsical or ludicrous aspects of prisoner-of-war life, we shared the same *raison d'être* for producing the work.

H.E. Woolley

Celebrating with close friends after wings parade, January 1941, Uplands Airport, Ottawa. Author, Frank Orme (killed in action), Jerry Mackay (killed in action).

CHAPTER ONE
For You the War is Over

P for Peter shadowed its way steadily over the North Sea, heading east towards the coast of Europe. As the Dutch coast drew steadily closer, Bill Robinson, the navigator, took a drift sight on the Texel beacon and discovered that the wind had thrown our aircraft slightly off course. Our meteorological briefing had advised of wind speed and direction which had been used to calculate our course to Bremen. However, the wind force had been underestimated by the meteorological "boffins," those scientists who supplied us with our crucial weather briefing. If we were to stay on track and avoid the fighter base at Leeuwarden a course correction would be necessary. Bill did a quick calculation and called up Snowdon the first pilot. "Alter course to 148° true, skipper. We're drifting too far north."

The crew of *P for Peter* was rather a mixed bag operating from RAF Squadron 115 situated near King's Lynn in Norfolk. John Snowdon, the pilot, was an RAF regular with several years of pre-war flying experience, and considerably senior in years to the rest of us. The other two Englishmen were Bill Robinson, navigator/bomb aimer and Peter Darvil, rear gunner. Alan Clarke, from Newfoundland, was wireless/airgunner situated in the front turret of the Wellington aircraft. The remaining members of the crew were Percy Brazier, wireless operator from Bracebridge, Ontario and myself as co-pilot.

It was a novel situation in which I found myself. Actually, I was a member of another crew and had volunteered to fill in at the last moment. I had been introduced, that afternoon, to John Snowdon, but had not met the other members of the crew. Prior to briefing I buttonholed Snowdon and asked him to show me the fueling system of a Mark VI Wellington. He testily suggested I find a ground crew aircraft fitter to go over it with me. Like most multi-engined aircraft, the fuel tanks could feed either or both engines, and the flow of petrol could be diverted or re-routed by opening and closing valves as required. It was not complicated, but it was essential that the co-pilot be familiar with the system. How fortunate that I took the time to find out was to be proved very soon.

The bomber stream that night consisted of approximately three hundred aircraft, most of which were Wellingtons, together with a few Halifaxes and Whitleys. In late October 1941, the Wellington was the mainstay of Bomber Command, although by today's standards it was small and slow. As we droned eastwards we all drew some degree of confidence from

Elementary flying training class, Windsor Mills, Quebec, September 1940. Author is seventh from left.

the knowledge that we were not alone. All around us, above and below us, in the darkening skies, hid by heavy cloud, the stream of bombers was slowly converging on Bremen, the primary target.

As I stood amidships I watched our starboard wing dip slightly as the skipper altered our heading in response to the navigator's course correction. The crew of *P for Peter* were not to find out until months later that our decision to change course would prove fateful. Subsequent piecing together of events in conversation with other crews revealed that we were one of a very few to change course. The main body of the assault force continued on the original track, unaware of the wind shift until further inland. Although ours was a sound decision, it had the effect of isolating us from the main body of the attack force, unless other crews made similar course adjustments. The old adage "safety in numbers" applies to relatively lightly defended aircraft when the opposing night fighters are far more heavily armed. Although we did not know it, we were a sitting duck, and were being tracked by German radio direction-finding (RDF) stations on the ground.

Through scattered breaks in the cloud I had occasional glimpses of German rivers and small towns. The wretched practice of black-out regulations achieves very little benefit when the drop in civilian morale caused by gloomy black-outs is weighed against the dubious protection it affords. Any aircrew member will verify that even on dark nights it is virtually impossible to hide from a strike force. A ship at sea, by going dark, can remain undetected: a city or town - never!

Occasional puffs of flame and distant crumps of exploding anti-aircraft shells broke the otherwise darkened skies, and bore witness to the fact that enemy defences were alert. So far none had disturbed our relentless progress towards our target, as each crew member made final preparations for the final run-in on the railway marshalling yards of Bremen.

With devastating suddenness the quiet, efficient routines of last-minute preparations were shattered! As German cannon ripped into our starboard wing accompanied by Peter's excited "Bandits six o'clock and below!" I watched in semi-stupefied horror from the mid-upper turret as six streams of tracer from the enemy night fighter tore into us. The answering fire from Peter's two Brownings was pitifully insignificant, but more accurate than the merciless cannonading power of the four streams of heavy calibre fire, plus two supporting machine-guns. Had the German ME 110 pilot aimed more accurately we would have exploded in a giant fire-ball as our ruptured tanks spilled sheets of volatile petrol into the night. Desperately Snowdon fought to prevent a final death dive as *P for Peter* corkscrewed out of control and screamed towards the earth in a deadly inward spiral, exerting centrifugal G forces which made it extremely difficult to move. I heard Snowdon's command to close off the starboard fuel supply and get forward as quickly as possible. All his considerable strength was unable to pull our stricken aircraft out of its final dive. From our operating height of four thousand metres we had dropped twenty-five hundred in a few seconds and my added weight on the control column was desperately required by the gasping, struggling pilot. With difficulty I fought my way past Percy who was at his post and signalling a Mayday, past Bill Robinson at his navigating instruments, and lurched into the cockpit beside the sweating, cursing Snowdon. His face was contorted by the herculean efforts, and he was scarcely able to gasp a plea for help as he fought the controls. Somehow the two of us pulled *P for Peter* straight and level. "We're losing fuel skipper. I must shut down the flow of petrol to the starboard wing tanks." He nodded and I fought my way towards the control valves to seal off our rapidly diminishing fuel supply which was escaping through the torn and shattered wing which seemed to have disappeared. How Snowdon was able to prevent another spin attested to his skill and experience as an RAF old regular pilot.

Again I fought my way forward to free Alan Clarke from his front turret. We were now down to six hundred metres and Snowdon ordered us to prepare for possible bail out, but first Alan had to be freed from his trapped position or go down with Snowdon. Finally it was accomplished and Clarke crawled to the mid-section to join the rest of the crew who were in position to parachute.

"Jettison all bomb load!" Snowdon ordered, and the aircraft, freed of eighteen hundred kilograms of incendiaries, lurched sluggishly upward and became more manageable. It was now possible to hold course at 270° and maintain height. We might make it to the North Sea and ditch the aircraft. I watched in fascination as the darkened countryside exploded into blinding light as our bomb-load ignited on the ground. I shall never know whether our load set empty fields blazing or whether a town or village was set on fire.

With a hundred and sixty kilometres to go to reach the Dutch coast, *P for Peter* fought its way westward. Both my feet were braced on the instrument panel. My added strength was needed as Snowdon tired in his desperate fight to keep us airborne. The fuel gauge which showed over three-quarters empty added to our concern.

Reaching England was out of the question. Our only hope now was to make it to the sea, to be picked up by the Dutch. Our one remaining engine continued to hold us on a roughly accurate bearing of due west. The Wellington aircraft was well designed and capable of maintaining height with one engine

15

gone. Freed of our bomb-load we were able to gain a little height and approached the Dutch border at twelve hundred metres. No one spoke as we struggled stubbornly across Holland: a stricken aircraft, almost completely defenceless, incapable of evasive action should another fighter strike. And then our faithful port engine began to falter as the fuel tank emptied. Snowdon throttled back and the engine, now on reduced power, picked up; but lacking sufficient speed, *P for Peter* was losing height at a rapid rate. We were over the coast but could see the cold North Sea awaiting us. "Check the dinghy, and prepare for ditching!" ordered Snowdon. We slid over a small island and again were the target of enemy fire from anti-aircraft installations. I ducked instinctively as the tracer shells tore through the fuselage. Miraculously no one was hit - but *P for Peter* was finished. At zero metres we wallowed at close to stalling speed. At the very last moment a lighthouse rushed toward us. Snowdon yanked the control column and it passed below us, by some miracle. We stalled and sank into the waiting sea with a series of bouncing, skipping crashes as we slowly lost speed. I have no recollection of the next few seconds. I was torn from my post and thrown forward, to be buried in cold, wet sand as the Wellington came to a screeching wrenching stop on tidal flats. For a few seconds all was deathly quiet. "Get out quickly!" Snowdon's cool voice did not have to repeat the order. "Is everyone all right?" "I can't move," I responded. My head was free but my body, although apparently unhurt, was unable to free itself. The crew of *P for Peter* rallied gallantly to free their trapped co-pilot from the wet clinging sand and mud and scrambled quickly from the mid-section.

Snowdon's first two thoughts were for the dinghy and for the classified IFF "black box" which must not be allowed to fall intact into enemy hands. "Someone get the dinghy out and destroy the IFF," he ordered. I sprang back into the ditched

16

aircraft, seized a fire axe and quickly pounded the mechanism to pieces. I then attacked the instrument panel and made short work of altitude indicator, compass, altimeter and various other potentially useful indicator dials. The dinghy I pushed out onto the wing and quickly rejoined the group.

There then followed one of those strange occurrences which attest to the sense of propriety and protocol of the English. John Snowdon, on a strange beach scarcely half a kilometre from a German anti-aircraft battery, with the stricken aircraft as background, solemnly made a formal introduction of his co-pilot to the crew. As I shook their hands I couldn't help but wonder at what manner of people they were who observed the niceties amid the confusion and fire of war.

Quickly we took stock of our situation. If we could manhandle the inflated dinghy into deeper water we faced an open sea voyage of nearly three hundred and twenty kilometres to reach England. The only other alternatives were to await the arrival of Germans from the flak station or to attempt to evade capture by splitting up and trying to escape on our own. We had to make our decision quickly. It would only be a matter of minutes before we were found by the German garrison who must have witnessed our final moments. Snowdon made his choice quickly. "All hands to the dinghy!" We sprang to action, seized our life-raft and started for the sea on the double. We had to make the attempt since it was the duty of downed aircrew to evade capture as long as possible. The prospect of an open sea voyage in an unprotected rubber dinghy in early November across the stormy North Sea was definitely not a pleasant one. I looked back at our downed aircraft. The sight of its gaunt bullet-riddled fuselage, the now still propellers and its tail fin pointing starkly skywards drove home to me the finality of the situation.

The silence of the night was broken as two streams of enemy machine-gun fire opened up on us. The red tracer shells converged on a point which effectively boxed us in and prevented any further prospect of escaping across the North Sea. Over the sands a contingent of Germans from the flak station advanced towards us. We could hear their voices as they exchanged information in German and quickly located our position. "Hande hoch!" We looked directly down the barrels of half a dozen sub-machine-guns manned by very young-looking German troops in the grey-blue uniform of the German air force who manned the anti-aircraft batteries. We raised our hands and were led off by our captors under the leadership of an officer with the rank of major.

The island was called Schiermonnikoog (the Isle of the Grey Monk) and formed part of the West Fresian Islands which run down the coast of Holland. As we were led inland we approached a heavily reinforced door which appeared to have been set directly into the side of a hill. The German major spoke a command and we were led through this door which closed behind us. We were allowed to lower our hands and found that we were in a sort of large underground canteen with corridors leading off it, which appeared to lead to sleeping quarters. Now that we had been safely rounded up, the attitude of the guards became more relaxed. The major, a roly-poly sort of individual, was almost jovial. No doubt it was a feather in his cap to have captured the entire crew of a British bomber!

Beer and schnapps quickly began to flow as our grinning captors saluted us and invited us to join them in toasting the fortunes of war. Under ordinary circumstances it would have had the potential of developing into a bang-up drunk. The Germans were in good form and eager to salute fallen enemy warriors. We had reason, too, to be thankful. We were alive

18

and unhurt, and should have been eager to join our enemies in an evening of drinking. However, after the first drink we exchanged warning glances. With apparent acceptance of the situation, we seized upon every opportunity to spill our drinks on the floor or to otherwise dispose of the liquor, all the while maintaining an outward appearance of camaraderie. We were careful to give nothing more than our names, ranks and service numbers and to keep our minds clear and alert.

The major was in excellent spirits, looking forward to the following morning and the pleasure of delivering six enemy aircrew into the custody of the German authorities. He positively beamed with pleasure, and as drink followed drink he became wildly exuberant. My high-school German was pressed into use, and I was able to ascertain that we would sleep there and be transported by ferry across the Zuider Zee in the morning to the Dutch mainland. Beyond that we did not care to speculate on our eventual fate. Since it was quite evident that this would be our last chance to enjoy any form of relaxed or sociable drinking, we perhaps would have been excused if we had allowed ourselves to be swept along by the general air of revelry. The long evening eventually wore on to the inevitable conclusion. The major slid off his chair about 3:00 am and was carried off, while we exchanged thankful glances and allowed ourselves to be paraded off to sleep by the remaining drunken guards still capable of navigation.

As tired and emotionally drained as we were, none of our crew was able to get any sleep; events had moved too quickly and savagely, and our adrenalin was still flowing. Promptly at seven o'clock we were awakened and herded unwashed into a truck which moved off bumpily. Two armed guards sat stonily at the rear. The trip was very short, and within a few minutes we were drawn up on a pier alongside a ferry boat which was taking on passengers. Most of the travellers were Dutch

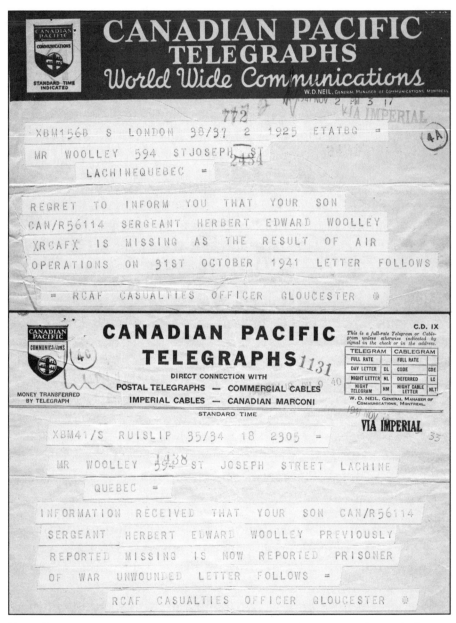

Two telegrams received by the author's parents. The first reports him missing on operations. In the second, received sixteen days later, he is reported POW.

housewives with shopping bags, going over to the mainland for such limited grocery shopping as was available in wartime Holland. Our morale was somewhat raised by the furtive waves and shy smiles which these Dutch matrons gave us whenever a guard was not looking. News of our sudden arrival the previous evening had obviously gotten around.

The ferry boat ride took about two hours to reach the Dutch fishing village of Harlingen. During the trip the German officer in charge decided to relieve John Snowdon of his prized sheepskin flying jacket. There was a promise that he would return it when it had been searched, but clearly it was merely to quieten the Englishman who was furious over the loss. When we were transferred from the ferry to another truck Snowdon was still bristling and demanding that it be returned. He might just as well have asked for an interview with Adolf Hitler, since it was obvious that his jacket would never be seen by him again. The German *oberleutnant* had a discriminating eye; he spotted a blue silk scarf which I wore under my zippered flying suit and quickly appropriated that as well, as a justifiable spoil of war. We were certainly in no position to argue and arrived at the Dutch aerodrome near Leeuwarden feeling thoroughly demoralized.

Our morale was not improved when we were ushered into a sort of aircrew ready room and introduced to a grinning *Luftwaffe* officer who claimed to be the ME 110 pilot who had attacked us the night before. He was, of course, most pleased with himself, and justifiably so, since an enemy kill under night flying conditions requires a large degree of skill and coordination between ground and air defences. Our next visitor was an intelligence officer who asked the usual questions and received the only information we were permitted to give. The interview was short and perfunctory. Although for the time being we had gotten off lightly, it was quite plain that the German interrogation had only just begun, and we would be subjected to more intensive questioning later on.

Once again we were loaded onto a small truck with benches down either side. There was just enough room to sit facing each other with an armed guard seated on each side nearest the tail-gate. Through gaps in the canvas cover we could snatch the occasional glimpse of the flat Dutch countryside as we sped quickly and recklessly along with much swaying and bumping around. Slowly the countryside began to change, and we were now in the suburbs of a large town. The German driver continued his hair-raising display, and actually appeared to be enjoying himself as startled pedestrians jumped clear to avoid this mad driver. Some of the bolder ones shook their fists as they recovered their equilibrium. The canals of Amsterdam would, under any other circumstances, have been charming and picturesque to contemplate, but under these conditions we were relieved when the truck drew up to a swerving, screeching halt in front of the city jail on a sunny November morning in 1941. It was a formidable and dreary looking edifice with heavily barred windows. The cell blocks were dark, and most of them seemed to be occupied by dozing inert figures who made no effort to look up as we were marched by. One by one we were deposited into cells. Never shall I forget the awful finality of the clang of the steel door as it closed, leaving me alone with my thoughts.

CHAPTER TWO
Adventures With Wire-Cutters

In the early days of our prisoner-of-war existence the desire to escape assumed varying degrees of importance among the men. To some it was an all-consuming passion. The confines of the barbed wire were unbearable to men like these, who could not rest while any plan of escape which contained even a glimmer of hope remained untried. Others of us, of a more philosophical nature, or perhaps less adventurous, were content to adapt to the situation, to make the best of it, to wait it out and accept the relative security of camp life in preference to the unknown but very real dangers of escape attempts.

Although there were various methods used to "slip the surly bonds" of prison camp existence, restricted only by the daring and ingenuity of the men who tried them, there were essentially only two methods. The most common was, of course, the tunnel. The quickest was by cutting through the double rows of barbed wire - plus the coils of tangled wire between - under the noses of the sentries in the "goon boxes" which stood at intervals around the perimeter. It was extremely dangerous even by night and virtually impossible by day. The wire was swept by searchlights and patrolled by guard dogs, which heightened the odds against success. Nevertheless it was not impossible and for this reason, if one was considering such an attempt, it was necessary to acquire a strong, reliable pair of wire-cutters.

I personally knew of two attempts. The first was made from Stalag VIII B by the redoubtable Red Gordon and John Snowdon in the winter of 1941/42, and was successful. The two men made a daring dash through the wire and got clear of the camp, only to be returned a week or so later almost frozen but undaunted. The second was a solo attempt by Teddy Joyce from Stalag Luft III. Despite our attempts to create a diversion, Joyce was machine-gunned before our eyes and died on the wire.

Since it was considered one's duty to attempt escape, my early months of captivity were devoted to attempts to acquire a pair

A group of Canadian Air Force prisoners at Stalag VIIIB, Lamsdorf, November 1941. This was an official photograph provided by the Germans. Author is fourth from the right in the third row.

of wire-cutters. A young Englishman, named John Bowden, and I had a half-formed plan which was more or less in limbo pending the acquisition of the precious pair of snippers. The old adage that "everything has its price" was no exception in prison camp, and eventually, by making the necessary sacrifices and with some help from a go-between, I was able to purchase the wire-cutters.

Having gone to so much trouble and expense in acquiring them you would naturally suppose that great care would be taken to ensure their safe keeping. My first adventure was due largely to carelessness on my part. The roaming German "ferrets" who slid quietly into barracks from time to time in the hopes of coming upon contraband items were rarely successful. It was the practice to post look-outs whose duty was to warn us of their approach. The cry of "bandits in the hut" frequently warned us to hide any maps, timetables, tools, or documents.

I had retrieved my wire-cutters from the bottom of my straw mattress to make some repairs to the heels of my worn flying boots. The claw pincers were useful to rip off the almost worn-out heel, and to pull out the nails which fastened the heel to the boot. So engrossed was I in my job I missed the warning cry "bandits in the hut." My first indication of danger was the weight of a heavy paw on my shoulder, and a triumphant gold-capped toothy grin accompanied by the reeking odour of garlic sausage as the ferret reached out and relieved me of my pincers. He shoved the long-handled tool through his belt and planted his feet apart, laughing delightedly while I cursed myself for my carelessness. The rest of the chaps were sympathetic but could do little to help as the guard continued to chuckle and enjoy his moment of triumph.

I continued to gaze at my lost wire-cutters with helpless fascination. At all costs I must recover them. But how? The

Greeting card sent from Stalag VIIIB in 1941.

guard was armed and completely in control of the situation. I would no doubt hear from the escape committee, too, for having been so careless with valuable property. I had to do something! The slender handles of the wire-cutters protruded from the top of the leather belt of the guard as he rocked on his heels with hands on hips, a satisfied look of smug arrogance on his face. Sensing my thoughts, one of the chaps held out a package of fags, offering one to the ferret who greedily accepted the cigarette and reached for his lighter. Now was my chance! My eyes were rivetted on my wire-cutters and the compulsion to make a lunge for them was overwhelming. While the guard, with the evident intention of adding a satisfying puff of an English cigarette to crown his little *coup*, applied lighter to cigarette, my hand reached out and snatched the handles. I wrenched them free, turned, and took off running. A sprinter out of the starting blocks in the hundred metre dash would have been hard pressed to better my take-off as I dashed madly for the door. I was half way down the barracks before the dumbfounded German guard knew what had happened!

I flew out the door clutching the wire-cutters, swung in a half turn and entered the adjoining hut. The ferret was now in pursuit and emerged from the hut in time to see me disappear into the next barrack, but fear gave wings to my feet and as I raced through the building I was already planning my next move. Instead of turning left to enter another hut I turned right and rushed back to my own. By the time the German emerged and looked distractedly about I was nowhere to be seen! He was by now feeling rather foolish and, obviously unwilling to face the amused inhabitants of hut 57A, he shuffled off and disappeared through the main gate.

I lay panting under a bunk waiting for the sound of heavy jackboots to come thundering through the barracks. The amused inhabitants of the hut eventually assured me that it was safe to emerge from my hiding place, and I rather sheepishly returned to my own bunk and hid the tool safely away. I hoped that the ferret had not taken the time to get a close look at me. It was not likely that in a camp of over five hundred men he would recognize me. To be on the safe side, however, I carefully kept out of his way whenever he was in camp.

The second incident concerning my wire-cutters occurred when we were moved from Lamsdorf to Stalag Luft III near Sagan, and demonstrates a rather remarkable facet of the German soldier's intellect. German army discipline was harsh, and blind obedience to the very letter of any command was expected. The German soldier's strict adherence to duty came

Unteroffizier **Kussel, the most hated guard in the RAF sector of Stalag VIIIB. Photograph was taken through a hole in a battle dress jacket.**

first above all. *Befehl est Befehl* was his creed: duty is duty. When it came to his duty he possessed a sort of tunnel vision, excluding all other extraneous thoughts and would have unquestioningly marched into a pool of alligators if ordered to do so. The fact that a safe bridge across might be only ten feet to his right would be irrelevant. His orders were clear and beyond question.

A move to a new camp was an opportunity for Jerry to uncover contraband items. We had somehow to get them through extremely exhaustive security measures, including the most intimate body searches. Our personal belongings were scrutinized, held up to strong lights, carefully prodded for unusual lumps, and subjected to rigorous appraisal. The slightest cause for suspicion and the offending article was confiscated. My own immediate concern was how to successfully get a largish pair of wire-cutters with fifty-centimetre handles through the search.

We marched in ranks of five to the large barrack just outside the main gate at Stalag VIII B, Lamsdorf, where the search was to be conducted. I was attempting to keep in step which was made more difficult by having to throw my left leg forward without bending the knee. This was due to the pair of handles shoved into my boot and acting as a sort of splint. No one gave much hope for my chances of getting away with it. However, I still hàd one card to play and would do so when the moment arrived.

Search procedure was simple. In groups of fifty or so we passed through the main gate under heavy guard, entered the large empty barrack, removed all of our clothes, and stood naked as plucked chickens while flashlights were shone in embarrassing places. Our clothes were subjected to minute inspection and our personal equipment equally thoroughly examined. Finally we were allowed to dress, reformed into fives and herded into freight cars for the trip to Sagan.

As my group entered the search area my mood was part philosophical and part grim determination. I would accept the outcome, but would not meekly hand over my symbol of defiance, which, in reality, was what my wire-cutters had become. The order to strip was given and fifty men

My dearest Wynne,

March 31 1943

I haven't received any mail from you for quite some time now. The last one was dated November 29 and was addressed to Geneva. Once again I want to thank you for cabling my folks. I should have known anyway that it was just the thoughtful kind of thing you would have done. You mentioned the Red Cross and said you were sending a parcel. Honestly Wynne — and I really mean it — you mustn't do these things. I sincerely hope you haven't spent any money just to send me things. I already owe you such a lot which will take me a long time to repay. I miss you terribly Wynne, and the hope that you are waiting for me makes it a thousand times more bearable here. As I have said before I get lots of thinking time here, and I am more certain than ever that my feelings towards you haven't altered a tiny bit. I see my folks have been writing you. I hope you haven't discovered things about my misspent past which shows you the kind of boy I really am. On second thoughts I don't suppose you have or you wouldn't still be writing me. We are now just beginning to enjoy lovely spring weather here. It shouldn't be long before things happen — I sincerely hope. I wish I had ten more pages like this so I could ask you half the things I'd like to. Don't forget to give my love to your Mum, Edie and Anne. Bye bye and all my love dear, Ted.

Letter to fiancée from Stalag VIIIB. German authorities permitted two such letters per month.

commenced the undignified process. Owing to a typhus epidemic we had all been subjected to head shaving so the situation was not without humour. To be naked before fully clothed and armed soldiers is embarrassing. To be naked and devoid of hair is beyond that. The last scraps of pride and self-respect seem to melt away. The only recourse is to refuse to take the matter seriously. We quickly assumed an attitude of amused enjoyment of the whole rather ludicrous situation and the search commenced amid ribald comment and somewhat forced laughter on our part while the guards did their part with solemn thoroughness.

As I removed the last of my clothes I very deliberately, and with no attempt to hide my actions, leaned the large pair of wire-cutters against a post in the middle of the search area. Several eyebrows were raised as my comrades saw what I was doing, but they quickly recovered themselves and pretended not to notice anything unusual. As the guards proceeded with the searching it seemed incredible that the large pair of wire-cutters could possibly go unnoticed. In addition to the actual searchers there were German guards standing stolidly around, indifferently overseeing the process. If their eyes did fall upon the wire-cutters they did not appear to register an awareness of anything unusual. They had their orders. Anything which required initiative of any sort beyond the clearly obvious directive to guard the prisoners was beyond them.

The entire search operation could not have lasted more than twenty-five minutes. To me it seemed an eternity. How long could the offending pair of snippers possibly go unnoticed? There they lay completely visible to all! Surely it would only be a matter of time until a searcher noticed them as they leaned starkly against the concrete pillar. The dull black handles stood out like a black stork on a garden lawn after the first fall of snow. The suspense was becoming unbearable. Finally we were ordered to dress. I kneeled down close to the white pillar and laced up my boots. I fumbled nervously with the laces, took a quick look about me, jammed the tool into my boot heel, pulled on my worn trousers and stood up, half expecting a heavy hand to fall on my shoulder: but nothing happened!

We marched from the barrack and headed to the line of waiting boxcars. Not until I was safely aboard did I dare to believe that I had pulled it off.

The guards had done their duty and carried out exhaustive search procedures as they had been ordered to do. With single minded thoroughness, all packages, clothing and equipment had been rigorously examined. The fact that a large pair of forbidden wire-cutters had stood unnoticed says much about the blind adherence to duty that typified the ordinary foot-soldier of the German forces. It makes for interesting speculation on the relative merits of blind obedience versus displays of initiative bordering on insubordination, behaviours at the opposite poles of military philosophy.

CHAPTER THREE
Ian

He was slightly built - the type of person who would never
stand out anywhere. It was incredible to realize he had been
pilot of a Manchester bomber aircraft. He could, if he wished,
have told as gripping a tale as any one of his comrades of his
bail-out from a fiery aircraft and eventual capture. The
Manchester was a twin-engined aircraft which was supposed to
have made the old reliable Wellington obsolete. It was,
however, to the bomber aircraft what the Edsel was to the
Ford motor car. It was a lemon, and hated thoroughly by all
who flew in her. It was his fate to experience firsthand its poor
manoeuvrability and inadequate fire-power in combat. He had
remained gallantly at the controls of his burning aircraft until
he was sure his crew had bailed out before saving himself.

I shall call him Ian. He was Scottish by birth and arrived at
Lamsdorf prison camp about a week after me in the fall of
1941. He was alone and scared when he was first admitted to
the RAF compound. It was a frightening enough experience to
meet the motley assortment of ex-fliers who greeted one at
this camp when armed with the moral support of one's own
crew members. Ian arrived without his crew, who showed up
later. He was shaken and nervous, and spoke little at first.
When he was given an upper bunk close to where I slept, he
bedded down immediately, shutting himself off from any
contact. Into the small hours of his first night I could hear an

occasional sob as he lay quietly with his face away from me. It was not unusual for sensitive boys to weep when first experiencing the harsh reality of prison camp. It was a form of catharsis for many of us who, having come so close to violent death, had been subjected to rough methods of interrogation, suffered various indignities and then been thrown into Stalag VIII B in the early winter of 1941. Most of the prisoners in the camp had been captured at Dunkirk and as army regulars made no secret of their dislike of air force blue. It was perhaps fortunate that the air force compound was separate from British army inmates who had been there well over a year already.

As the first few days passed Ian slowly emerged from his shell and began to join in. When the rest of his crew arrived his spirits rose considerably, but for some reason he preferred to mess on his own. Most of us pooled our meagre rations into "combines" or groups. Ian chose to go it alone.

At this stage of the war the prisoners existed largely on German rations. If an occasional Red Cross parcel issue was made, it was minute and usually shared among many. A parcel intended for one man for one week was shared six or even eight ways. Since it was difficult to distribute evenly such items as tins of condensed milk or cans of soup, we usually drew lots for the contents, which had been broken into items of roughly equivalent value.

As the days went by a new side of Ian emerged. He was a compulsive horse trader. He simply could not resist the urge to swap and barter away his Red Cross or German issue. It was quite common to engage in this practice, and on parcel issue day many of us swapped our bar of chocolate for a tin of jam, or obtained a ration of powdered milk in exchange for a German ration of bread which was fifty per cent sawdust and fifty per cent black flour of some kind. Ian, however, was obsessed with a desire to wheel and deal which went far beyond the normal limits of barter and which got him involved with contraband items such as compasses, wire-cutters and warm clothing. Before long he had acquired a reputation and was generally approached first when one was out of razor blades or needed wool to darn a sock. He usually was able to come up with the required item.

Ian, however, lacked the one essential ingredient of successful entrepreneurs. He had no business sense whatever. He operated out of the sheer need to be part of the action, and left so many loose ends and half-completed deals hanging in mid-air that his affairs very quickly became chaotic. In his insatiable need to swing deals he very often was taken advantage of by some of the more unscrupulous men who sensed an opportunity to profit from his consuming desire to please. In civilian life, if he had had an efficient assistant to keep his affairs in order, and perhaps even give advice to him, he may have been successful, since he certainly possessed drive and an almost phenomenal ability to produce the goods. As it was he very soon found himself in difficulties. In today's vernacular, he soon developed cash flow problems which necessitated belt-tightening measures to maintain solvency. He was frequently forced to forego his ration to satisfy urgent and immediate demands by clients who expected to be paid for services rendered. I am quite sure that had his customers realized just how deeply Ian was in debt they would never have pressed their claims so relentlessly.

There then occurred an event which brought the situation to a head. It was getting on towards Christmas. Most of the prisoners had been setting aside a small part of their Red Cross issue so that on Christmas day they could celebrate and enjoy a respite from the hunger pains which perpetually

35

gnawed at their empty stomachs. The senior NCO at this time was John Taylor-Gill, an RAF pilot much respected for his level-headedness. It had been reported to him that rations had been disappearing from the shelves where they were kept. At this time the camp was run largely on the honour system, since short of sleeping with one's food, there was no way of ensuring its safety. For this reason, pinching another man's food was considered the most heinous of crimes. I had already witnessed the army vengeance which had been wreaked on one unfortunate culprit. The guilty man, who had been caught red-handed, had been thrown into the large communal latrine, together with all his belongings, including blankets and change of clothes. He was then subjected to the taunts and ridicule of his army buddies, while he attempted to clean himself from the effects of his ordeal. It was a sight which, once seen, would never be forgotten.

It was important to deal justly and fairly with this problem. The Germans were not concerned with internal disciplinary measures. It was up to Taylor-Gill to deal with it, and to do so quickly. He decided to set a simple trap by keeping watch for the thief. It had to be organized very quietly to avoid arousing his suspicions. No additional security precautions would be taken, since to do so would alert our man. Instead, six reliable men were detailed to form the watch from lights out at eleven till first light the following morning.

For the next two nights nothing untoward occurred, but on the third night our hungry pilferer struck again. In the early hours of the morning, the silence was broken only occasionally by the scraping of wooden clogs on concrete floors as sleepy prisoners stumbled to the washroom to relieve the calls of nature and returned groggily to their interrupted slumbers. At 3 am all was quiet when the silent watcher sensed a moving figure heading quietly in the direction of the food storage cupboards.

His eyes could make out a smallish form lifting items and replacing them with extreme care. The ghostly figure was taking great pains to be quiet, but at the same time was obviously searching for something. At length he appeared to have found what he was looking for and began to creep quietly back to his bunk.

The jig was up! The barrack was flooded with light and the unfortunate thief stood revealed with the proof of his guilt. For a slice of bread and a few scraps of chocolate the luckless man stood exposed as the lowest form of prisoner-of-war life: a thief who would steal his fellow prisoners' rations. It was Ian! His efforts to pay off his insistent creditors had been too much for him to bear and he had resorted to this. It was now up to Taylor-Gill to decide what to do with him.

The following morning he summoned Ian and informed him of his decision. He was aware of Ian's difficulties, and to some extent sympathized, but stealing from fellow prisoners could not be condoned. Therefore he was to be placed on a delayed charge, to be effective when circumstances made it possible for due course of justice to be carried out, upon our eventual repatriation to England. He would not, he added, take any immediate disciplinary measure since the humiliation alone was in his opinion sufficient punishment for the shattered pilot to endure.

Taylor-Gill was more correct than he realized. Ian's utter disgrace was in his own eyes more complete than even his fellow prisoners allowed. Most of us felt sorry for the fellow. His dealings had not been dishonest. He had merely succumbed to the inevitable results of his bankruptcy, and had allowed his animal instinct for survival to overwhelm his basically honourable upbringing. He was, in addition, an extremely sensitive lad. The result was that he began to retreat within himself again, and refused to eat or communicate. His withdrawal was so absolute that we began to fear for his sanity, and even his life, when a straight-edged razor was discovered under his pillow. If Ian had only realized that we felt pity and to some extent understanding, not contempt, he might have rallied somewhat. As it was, his sense of shame overwhelmed him, and he sunk lower and lower into a slough of black despondency.

One late afternoon just before roll-call I noticed that Ian was not in his usual apathetic sprawl in his sleeping quarters where he had taken to spending almost all of his waking hours. As the German guards entered the gate and the whistles began blowing, the prisoners briskly began to assemble. I had a strangely unsettling premonition. Something was wrong, and it had to do with Ian. We had all taken an almost motherly interest in the poor fellow's predicament and it was not unusual to feel concern, particularly since the incident with the razor. This was different. The feeling was one of ill-omen, almost of dread. I left the hut. I was one of the last, but instead of turning left to join my fellow prisoners who were assembled on the parade-ground, I turned right and raced to the back of our barrack. I saw immediately what I had dreaded, what I knew within me had been only a matter of time in becoming reality. There lay Ian. His slight body was curled in a half-moon position as if trying to conserve warmth. Tightly knotted around his throat was a narrow woollen scarf. His face was dark, his tongue protruded, his eyes stared at me but showed no sign of recognition. I tore away the scarf and ripped open his collar. He immediately gasped and instinctively drew in air. I knew then he was still alive!

Ian had reached bottom. There was nowhere lower for him to go. Strangely, he began to recover. Once again Taylor-Gill showed his wisdom, his understanding, and his humaneness.

38

From somewhere he was able to procure a rather the
worse-for-wear guitar. The army men who had been in camp
since Dunkirk had organized a musical group and Taylor-Gill
had no doubt used his influence, as senior NCO, RAF
compound, to obtain a cast-off instrument, some sheet music
and instructions on how to play.

The interview between the compassionate fighter pilot and the
young bomber pilot did not last long. Ian emerged with the
guitar. His eyes had at last lost some of their look of apathy.
They mirrored a soul reprieved from a private hell. As gently
as we could, we encouraged him as he began to feel his way
slowly into a new, and what later was to become an abiding
interest. He had a certain amount of natural talent and as his
mastery over the instrument grew so did his return to full
participation in daily camp life. He was seldom without his
beloved guitar, and became part of a fledgling band when
musical equipment was obtained. Ian never looked back. His
guitar became his life. All of us who had watched him sink to
the depths and rise again felt nothing but happiness for him.
His triumph was to some extent ours. His new sense of
purpose was shared by us all.

I am quite certain that Taylor-Gill, in his sound judgement and
sense of decency, never did proceed with charges. Ian had,
after all, repaid his debt. He became part of a group of
musicians that brought pleasure to many. The scales were in
balance.

CHAPTER FOUR
Dear John Letters and Others

Letters from home and loved ones played an enormous part in the lives of all prisoners of war. They were the sole link with the outside world, and were all-important in reassuring the men that some sort of normal life still existed in a world turned upside-down by cruel conflict. Every letter was read and re-read. Every word was seized upon and studied for possible alternate meaning. Many on the home front had made arrangements with departing sons to use simple code. In my own case I had promised my parents that the first letter of each paragraph would indicate where I was located. Letters home referred to Winston Churchill and Josef Stalin as Aunt Winnie and Uncle Joe in poor attempts to fool the censors when mentioning military matters. The Germans must have been amused at the large numbers of prisoners who had so many relatives with identical names.

Censorship was strict and it was not unusual for letters to arrive home with most of the message blocked out. To a certain extent it was true of incoming mail as well. It was, therefore, important for those on the home front to weigh carefully what they wrote in their correspondence to their sons or husbands. Well meaning but thoughtlessly worded letters could have a large impact on morale. An unfortunate phrase here, a word misunderstood there, were often the cause of needless worry or concern. Since letters took weeks or even months to arrive and very often were received out of sequence or in batches, unfortunate misunderstandings were often the reason for needless mental anguish, both at home and in the camp.

The Dear John letter will always be a part of wartime correspondence. Some of them were cruel, some were merely thoughtlessly worded. Most of them had an element of humour and, provided they were someone else's mail, many were screamingly funny! The Dear John letter originally was the term applied to a short note breaking off an engagement, but eventually included all mail which contained impossibly inappropriate remarks. The following excerpts are, I think, classics.

> *Dear John,*
> *I'm sorry to have to tell you that I could not wait any longer and have married your father.*
> *Love Mother*

> *I understand the German girls are very friendly. I hope you are going to remain true to me.*

> *I hope you are getting enough exercise. Too much rich food combined with little activity is not good for you.*

The following letter was received by a POW who had written to thank a young lady for a pair of socks received in a Red Cross parcel which had included her address.

> *I am pleased you liked the socks. I would have preferred that someone on active service had received them though.*

> *Dear John,*
> *Keep your chin up!*

This oft-repeated phrase became rather overdone by well-meaning relatives and friends.

From fiancée to POW shot down early in the war:

> *Darling, I was so glad you were shot down before flying became dangerous.*

> *Joe is in Stalag Luft III. You should drop over and see him sometime.*

> *Dear John,*
> *I hope this reaches you in time for Christmas. I trust you will behave yourself and not drink too much.*

> *Have you seen "Gone With the Wind" yet?*

> *Dear John,*
> *I wrote you two weeks ago and received no reply so you will understand why I am dating someone else.*

> *I have always wanted to visit Germany. You are fortunate to be able to see it for nothing!*

> *Dear John,*
> *I am sorry dear, I love a soldier. I know you will understand.*

Letter received by an airman shot down nearly two years earlier:

> *You are going to be a father.*

> *Dear John,*
> *I suppose when you get home you will eat only sauerkraut and schnitzel.*

Please send me a photograph if you have a moment.

Letter received by three-year prisoner in early 1945:

Dear John,
I have just had a baby, but don't worry, the American officer is sending you cigarettes every week.

Letter received by prisoner who had learned some German in high school.

Aren't you glad you took German. It's always nice to know the language when you are abroad.

Can you buy beer over there or do they sell only wines?

If you get a chance please pick me up one of those cute Bavarian meerschaum pipes.

I see you are in a different camp now. Did you have a nice journey?

Joe has just joined the air force. He says he will never allow himself to be taken prisoner.

Prisoner-of-war dental care was non-existent. A decayed tooth was extracted if necessary, without freezing or anaesthetic.

Darling - please have your teeth fixed up while you can have it done for nothing.

Dear John,
I am going out with a soldier rescued from France. He says the air force let him down on the beaches of Dunkirk.

Darling I have found a fantastic new diet for losing weight, would you like me to send it to you?

I hope you are not eating too many eggs. You know they are not good for you.

I am thrilled to hear you do most of your own cooking. I'll bet you will be quite an expert chef when you return home.

I don't care much for wartime hair-styles. Are the German girls' much the same as ours?

Dear John,
I am still getting notices from your tailor. Please send the money so I can pay these bills.

You have just received a letter from the Department of National Defence. You have been called up for military service.

I hope you like this snapshot of me in my swim-suit.

Such photos, received by long-term prisoners who had not been within hailing distance of the fair sex for some time, were eagerly shared by sex-starved men and discussed with brutal frankness.

Dear John,
I hope you are having regular medical check-ups.

If you are ever near Heidelberg be sure to see "The Student Prince."

I am going to send you some cigarettes; please let me know what brand you prefer.

Kriegsgefangenenlager   Datum: 12.12.43.

Happy Birthday
SWEETHEART

Ted.

Home-made birthday card sent to England from East Prussia.

Prisoners of war did not enjoy the luxury of choosing a brand. In hard times a single cigarette was sometimes shared between three or four men.

And the classic:
> *Dear John,*
> *For you the war is over.*

CHAPTER FIVE
Flyers in Khaki

A collection of stories about prisoner-of-war life must contain frequent references to the subject of escape. After all, it was considered one's duty to engage in escape operations, either actively or in related activities. The actual break-out was generally only made possible by days of careful planning by many men engaged in a large number of varied trades. These necessary skills included forgery, tailoring, printing, counterfeiting, map making, make-up and disguise, et cetera. Other necessary work which required no particular skill could include those who were willing to volunteer their time for sentry duty, sand dispersal from tunnels, or singing groups with no particular talent other than the ability to drown out the noises made by such activities as radio calibration or even wire cutting.

One of the obstacles facing air force prisoners of war who desired to escape was the extreme difficulty in getting outside the barbed wire. Under Geneva Conventions regulations governing treatment of prisoners of war, the detaining power was not permitted to use those with the rank of sergeant or higher in working camps. This effectively precluded all air force prisoner personnel. British and Allied forces army personnel below the rank of sergeant, however, could be sent on working parties in farm country, or into salt-mines or wherever German powers could use them, provided the work

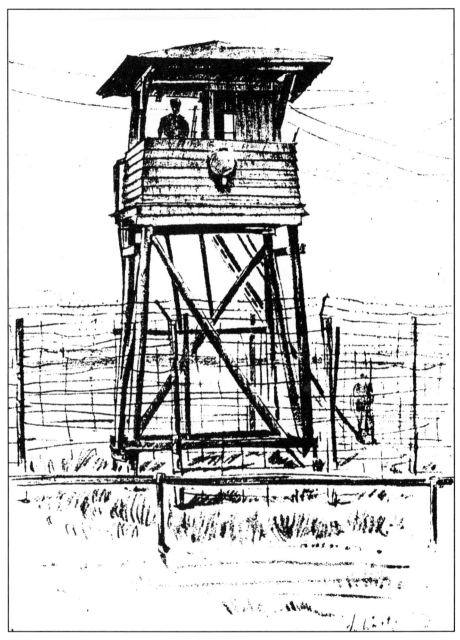

A POW's sketch of the German sentry box or "goon box."

was not directly related to the German war effort. (This was a moot point since it could be argued that it would be difficult to find any work which did not in some way contribute to the overall war effort.)

Escape from working parties was relatively easy, and air force prisoners looked with envy on their khaki-clad comrades who marched out of the camp to board transportation to the various work areas. A side benefit was the added opportunity to supplement meagre food rations by scrounging or bartering for fresh meat, eggs, and other farm produce which the countryside afforded.

In the winter of 1941/42 escape plans had to be postponed. It was a cruel winter in Europe, and the prospect of roaming around enemy territory half-frozen was not appealing even to the most determined of would-be escapers. With the coming of spring, however, we began to experience a curious phenomenon. Suddenly, and without our prior knowledge, strange faces began to appear on parade. In the barracks familiar figures disappeared and their bunks were occupied by strangers wearing air force blue answering to the names of the former occupants.

What was going on? Were we being infiltrated by planted informers? If this were so, Jerry was being rather obvious. The answer had to be something else. The senior NCO was quick to realize that some explanation was due since carefully planned escapes could be jeopardized unless everyone was put in the picture. One evening after roll-call he called for attention and placed sentries at each end of the barracks.

"Gentlemen," he began quietly. "You have no doubt noticed that something unusual is going on. Some of your buddies seem to have vanished while strangers have begun to appear

49

among us. You are not to let on to anyone, particularly the guards, that you are aware of anything unusual. You are to address these newcomers at all times by the names they have assumed. They are to be trusted. They are in fact British soldiers who have agreed to change identities with air force flyers. Please make these men welcome, but be careful not to do or say anything to arouse suspicion since this is only the beginning of a program to find ways of aiding escape. That is all, gentlemen."

So that was it! Air force personnel were switching identities with non-commissioned British soldiers in order to make their escape attempts from working parties in Germany, occupied Poland or Czechoslovakia. The actual switch had to be a carefully planned operation, since in Stalag VIII B the air force compound was actually a camp within a camp, separated from army personnel by barbed wire and situated in the centre of the camp. To get from the air force compound into the surrounding army camp was next to impossible without cutting through the guarded wire which separated them.

The Germans did permit football matches between air force and army teams. They also allowed spectators from the army compound to accompany the players when they visited the air force compound, and vice versa when the games were played on army territory. The visitors were, of course, always counted before leaving, marched under guard to the home team's football pitch, and counted again before being escorted home under guard. Curiously enough, while the actual game was in progress they made no attempt to stop friendly intermingling between the different branches of the services. Thus it was possible to carry out prearranged identity swaps during the course of the game. The two men who had previously made the arrangements would simply disappear into the latrine, exchange clothes, and carefully memorize identification data such as POW number, service serial number, and where they had been taken prisoner. At game's end, they would march back with their new comrades. The actual identity dog-tag which each prisoner wore was never exchanged. This precious item was the only piece of identification which positively identified one as a prisoner of war. It thus ensured that one was not jailed or shot as a saboteur or member of a resistance movement - occupations which carried a death sentence if one were caught.

It must be remembered that most army personnel had been captured at Dunkirk, and had therefore been prisoners for a year and a half. They could therefore be excused if their desire to escape had been blunted somewhat by the grim reality of its near impossibility. The urge to escape tended to decrease in an inverse ratio to the duration of captivity.

In the early summer of 1942, since I had been a prisoner just over six months, I was interested in any scheme of escape which might arise. The relative ease with which these identity swaps were being carried out accounted for the initial trickle of swap-overs to swell into an incoming tide of khaki and outgoing air force blue. Scarcely a day went by which did not find new faces appearing, and familiar ones no longer around.

Taffy Evans and I decided to have a go. Taffy was a sergeant wireless-operator from Bridgend, Wales. There were only two hurdles to get over before the actual exchange could be carried out. The first, and most obvious, was to find two army privates willing to make the switch. To accomplish this we merely approached the wire and, in guarded conversation with army personnel, let it be known that we wished to make the attempt, and agreed to make the arrangements on the next day with any volunteer. The second hurdle was to obtain permission from the escape committee. This was necessary so that poorly thought-out plans could be screened out. It was only a matter of time until Jerry caught on to what was happening, and the escape committee naturally wished to have some control over these wholesale changes, in order to postpone the clamping down which would inevitably occur. The blessing of the escape committee included a small supply of emergency rations and sometimes maps or compasses. At this stage, early in the war, such additional refinements as travel vouchers, forged papers, or identity cards were not available. The fact that I could manage a little German was in my favour. I could possibly pass as a Czech if picked up. The Czech border was scarcely thirty kilometres away and our goal was to make it there and hope to establish contact with their underground forces in Prague.

In a short interview Taffy and I received the okay to make the attempt. We had found two men captured at Dunkirk named Cooper and Baker who were willing to accommodate us at the next interservices football match. Neither Taffy nor I were aware of a third hurdle at this time and went busily about our preparations for the day of the next match which was in a week's time.

On the day of the match, which was to be held in one of the army compounds, Taffy and I were ready. At breakfast I spoke to my other crew members, informing them of my plans and requested that Private Cooper be shown my bunk on his arrival. They wished me luck and we shook hands. Shortly after lunch the football team and the forty odd spectators were formed up near the gate which led to the army compound. A detail of guards arrived to escort the party. The German NCO in charge did a quick count. We were fifty-seven in all, including team, spectators, one or two officials, and team handlers. Taffy and I were not empty-handed. We carried a minimum of personal effects and a carton containing some emergency rations. The guards were not unduly suspicious, as it was usual for a visiting football team to carry a few items of equipment in cardboard boxes. They glanced at the small packages and did not bother to open them for inspection as we passed through the gate into the army camp. So far so good!

It had been agreed beforehand that the quick change could wait until half-time. This was when the prisoners from the two services mixed and exchanged news and generally relaxed with a cigarette and a "brew up." The guards were used to this, and sometimes let down a little to join in the temporary respite from the day-to-day boredom to which they, as well as we, were subjected.

Cooper and Baker had shown up as promised, and nodded slightly in our direction as the contingent of air force prisoners came to a halt. We took up position on the perimeter of the football field - army supporters on one side, air force supporters on the opposite side. The standard of soccer was good and the match was well played. Both teams had a nucleus of former professionals from divisional levels in England. The air force team had the advantage of having been in captivity a shorter time, and consequently were in superior condition to the army players who had been in the camp for two winters.

At half-time players and spectators from both sides relaxed and exchanged news from England. The army lads relied on new air force arrivals for bits of home news, and if one was fortunate to find a newly-arrived flyer from one's home town it was an added pleasure. Interservice rivalry and army animosity towards air force tended to dissipate when the facts of Dunkirk were discussed openly and frankly by the men. After all, Air Marshall Dowding had pulled the air force from France to fight again another day, much as had Field Marshall Alexander with the army at Dunkirk. The unfortunate

Dunkirk prisoners could understand this in the light of later events.

Taffy and I did not have time for half-time socializing. As soon as the referee blew his whistle signifying the end of the half, we headed straight to the "kybo." This large latrine generally known by such affectionate names as "houses of parliament" or "reading room" was a large many-holed facility. It was the centre where ideas circulated, rumours originated, philosophical matters were discussed, and letters from home read again and again.

Cooper and Baker were already there. We did not exchange pleasantries. Cooper handed me a slip of paper with his POW number, service number, rank and the single word *Dunkirk*. Baker did the same to Evans. We quickly exchanged clothes. In the pocket of my battledress was a paper with my POW number, service number and the words *Sergeant Pilot, Bremen*. They wished us good luck. It crossed my mind to wish them a happy holiday, but I refrained. Instead we shook hands all round and made our way back to the football match. Fortunately we were all of medium build and as I joined the army lads on the far side of the field, I did not feel uncomfortable in my new uniform of khaki.

When the game ended, Taffy and I formed up with our new comrades to be marched back under guard to our new home which was in a separate compound, as was the air force camp. This made me a little uneasy since it meant another gate inspection when we entered. We had our precious boxes of escape rations with us. It would have been ironic if our plans were to be thwarted at the outset, and before we even got installed in our new quarters. My fears were justified. The guard at the gate immediately noticed my cardboard carton and headed straight for me. "Was haben sie da?" he asked, unslinging his rifle and prodding the flaps of the carton with the muzzle. I pretended not to understand and shrugged my shoulders and tried to look blank. The guard was in an ugly mood and began to scream at me to open the box. There was no future in pretending ignorance any longer. The guard screamed again, "Offnen sie!" I tried to register sudden comprehension and pulled open the flaps revealing a change of underwear, a shirt and socks covering the unopened cans. He grabbed one of the cans containing cod liver oil and malt and looked at it. This appeared to satisfy him. Since he obviously could not understand the label he seemed satisfied that it was a Red Cross tin of jam and grudgingly tossed it back and waved us through the gate. My pounding heart gradually returned to a normal beat. I wiped my arm across my forehead to clear the sweat and began to relax. We were safely in the army compound! Two of Cooper's mates directed us to our new sleeping quarters. The accommodation was identical to our own. Taffy and I were shown the top tiers of adjoining triple-decker bunks. Evening parade would be in two hours. We stretched out on the bunks and allowed the accumulated tension to slowly drain away and contemplated the situation.

For the next week or so we adapted ourselves to the new routine of army life. It was really no different from air force prisoner-of-war existence. The rations were the same, morning and evening parades were half an hour earlier. The evenings were spent either reading, playing cards, or listening to records received from England. The army sergeant major in charge of the hut read the BBC news in much the same manner as it was done in the air force enclosure with sentries posted at each end of the hut to warn of approaching guards.

As we entered the second week of our new life, we had heard no word from anyone about working parties. Spring was well advanced and conditions for escape as good as they would ever be. As soon as a suitable opportunity arose Taffy and I approached Sergeant Major Cox and asked him if he had a few moments to talk to us. Sergeant Major Cox was probably in his late thirties, a regular with the Gordan Highlanders who obviously took pride in his appearance. His brass buttons gleamed, his army boots shone, his worsted khaki tunic and trousers might well have been returned from a dry-cleaners that same day. The trousers were neatly tucked into army gaiters which also covered the tops of his gleaming boots. His entire bearing commanded the respect of prisoners and guards alike. We were slightly in awe of him. Technically we were of equal rank, but to Taffy and me barely twenty years of age, he seemed more of a father figure than a comrade-in-arms.

"I expect you know what we have come to you about," I began.

Sergeant Major Cox smiled and nodded his head. "Sit down," he said and made room on the wooden bench which stood before the table in front of his bunk. He sat down facing us on the opposite bench.

"We have an escape committee here just as I'm sure you have in the air force compound," he began. "All escape plans are cleared with them. This is essential if we are to maintain any sort of control and to arrange for cover for escapees. Unfortunately there are rare occasions when someone decides to carry out his plans without consulting anyone." Sergeant Major Cox pushed a tin containing excellently rolled home-made cigarettes towards us. Taffy and I shook our heads. He lit one for himself and took a moment or two before continuing. He appeared to be searching for the right words.

"Did you men have the opportunity to speak to Cooper and Baker before the actual identity exchange on the day of the football match?" Cox asked.

A typical camp latrine. This was a "forty holer" at Stalag VIIIB.

"Only a short conversation across the fence about a week before," I replied. "We told them we wished to get into the army compound as soon as possible, and they both agreed to switch identities on the next interservices football match."

"Did you tell them why you wished to swap over?" Cox asked.

"No," I said. "We naturally assumed they knew we wanted to attempt escape from a working party. It's the whole reason for the large-scale switches which are taking place."

"Well that's unfortunate," Cox went on, "because I'm afraid I have some bad news for you. Cooper and Baker have good army records. They were taken prisoner after serving with honour with the BEF at Dunkirk. Unfortunately, they have a record of trouble-making on the previous working parties in Silesia to which they were assigned by the Germans. They are no longer permitted by Jerry to leave the camp for any reason whatsoever. Although I approve of their conduct of being a thorn in the side of our captors, I think they acted irresponsibly in agreeing to switch identities with you without telling you these facts. They also failed to notify our escape committee of their plans."

Taffy and I were stunned. We had been hoodwinked by the pair of them who had been interested only in getting a change of scenery! We had successfully got over the first two hurdles only to find that a third and insurmountable hurdle stood in the way of our plan.

Sergeant Major Cox was sympathetic and continued. "Since I feel responsible as senior NCO here, I feel that I should give you whatever assistance I can. You cannot get on a working party and this leaves you with only two choices. You can remain as you are, or you can arrange to return to the air force camp. If you wish to follow the latter course I will order Cooper and Baker to cooperate at the first available opportunity."

Taffy and I were both in agreement. We would reluctantly scrap our present escape plan and return to life in the air force camp. Cooper and Baker had no choice, and on the day of the next interservice game the entire procedure was re-enacted. The switch went smoothly. At half-time we met and changed back into air force blue. The latrine was busy that day. On the same operation were two more army exchanging with two aircrew. As the eight of us hastily completed the change-over I wished the outbound aircrew better luck than we had had.

But the wholesale exchanges of identity eventually had to come to an end. The German authorities could not be fooled indefinitely. Unsuccessful escape attempts by air force personnel from army working parties revealed their true identities upon recapture. The camp security was tightened and prisoners were photographed and given identity cards. As time went on, the number of swap-overs dwindled until only a handful remained. But some of the effort had not been in vain. A small number of men had made it home to England. Others had remained in Europe and been absorbed by underground or resistance forces.

It had been a good effort and for quite some time had given German security its share of headaches, and used up valuable manpower sorting it all out.

Confused relatives in England and allied countries could once again look forward to letters from loved ones in Germany. The Red Cross had been attempting to reassure them that the strange correspondence from Germany in familiar handwriting but signed by apparent strangers was no cause for worry. To allay their fears they had been let in on the scheme. Nevertheless it must have been reassuring to anxious wives and sweethearts to once more be receiving letters from Sergeant Pilot Jimmy Jones signed by his real name and not "with all my love, William" from Private Willam Smith of the Gordon Highlanders.

CHAPTER SIX
I'm Twenty-One Today

> *I'm twenty-one today, twenty-one today.*
> *I've got the key of the door,*
> *Never been twenty-one before;*
> *Father said I could do as I liked,*
> *And I shouted "hip hooray!"*
> *Hey diddley hey,*
> *I'm twenty-one today!*

This old English music-hall number refers to a major milestone in the life of a boy who achieves his age of majority. He can now lawfully be served beer in a pub, is allowed to vote, and is now fully responsible for his actions. Nowadays the significance of reaching twenty-one is lost in a faster-paced life-style, when eighteen years of age or even sixteen brings the same privileges and responsibilities.

The ethics of each point of view could be argued with some merit. Perhaps we are more realistic today in allowing boys to do legally what they will probably do anyway. I have always thought that laws which allowed a young man to die for his country, but did not permit him to vote or be served a beer had a hypocritical aspect to which I have never been able to reconcile myself.

Official German photo features a group of Canadians at Stalag Luft III, Sagan. Later in the war this camp was the site of *The Great Escape*. Author in middle row, second from right.

My own twenty-first birthday occurred in October of 1942 when I had been a prisoner of war for nearly a year. The camp, Stalag Luft III, was comprised largely of RAF with a sprinkling of Canadians, Poles, Czechs, Australians, New Zealanders and Americans. The English, at this time, attached a great deal of importance to a twenty-first birthday, and usually marked the occasion by presenting a symbolic key of the door to the young man who had arrived at this momentous day.

In peacetime the large silver foil-covered key, suitably decorated with ribbons, was presented with all due ceremony by the proud father to the sometimes embarrassed offspring. As the cake was cut and the corks popped from champagne bottles, suitable speeches were made, and toasts were proposed wishing the young man well, and reminding him of his newly won responsibilities.

The ceremony in Stalag Luft III was, in its own way, equally elaborate. First of all it was necessary for the young man to make it known that his twenty-first was approaching by casually mentioning the fact to his closest friends. With carefully placed offhand remarks he made certain that all interested parties were informed of his approaching birthday.

On the appropriate day the senior NCO, Sergeant Pilot James Deans, would hold the men on parade after the German officer in charge had dismissed the men. Sergeant Deans nearly always did this, since there were usually announcements of interest and concern to the prisoners which he held until the camp authorities had made their twice-daily head count. In front of five hundred or so men, smiling approvingly, the young man was called to the centre of the parade-ground. Dixie, as James Deans was known, would bend and retrieve a key from where it had been buried in the dirt and solemnly make the presentation.

Perhaps you might think it a little thing. What's so special about a twenty-first birthday? I suppose if I were young in today's world where teenagers are far more blasé and sophisticated than we could ever hope to have been, I might view the situation differently. In an era that has seen widespread use of the pill, the emergence of civil rights, women's rights, gay liberation, trial marriage, permissiveness, firsthand television coverage of world-wide violence and unrest, and a drug culture of unimagined proportions, the simple act of recognizing a boy's coming of age may appear to be a trivial event.

Perhaps we who were locked behind wire barricades attached undue importance to small events. It is certainly true that unless we made a determined effort to rise above the barrenness of our existence, the days could be empty and unending, the evenings a procession of endless bridge games, of parcheesi, chess, checkers and poker for cigarettes, when frayed tempers and close association with the same old unshaven faces often resulted in bickering and fruitless arguments. It is well known that one of the major difficulties of space travel, arctic exploration or any project which requires living in close and protracted proximity can be clashes of personalities, leading to serious consequences. Anything that gave these high-spirited, restless men a temporary escape from routine was a welcome occurrence. The recognition of a twenty-first was such an event, and was given its full due.

I made certain that George, my messing partner from the British army who had been captured at Dunkirk, was made fully aware of my impending birthday. I did have doubts about George's reaction, since he was a hard-bitten, tough English coal-miner from Stoke on Trent who had little time for the social niceties. He had been an army boxer and his upper arms were vividly tattooed with daggers dripping blood. Once or twice he had put on the gloves with me to teach me the finer points of self-defence and had momentarily succumbed to the temptation of my inadequate defence, flooring me and knocking me senseless, for which he had immediately and profusely apologized. I had seen him knock a Czech pilot clean across the room with one crushing blow during a fight over cooking space on the one small stove which served the hut. He was a man not to be fooled with.

For these reasons I had definite doubts about his attaching much importance to my impending birthday. Nevertheless as the eighth day of October 1942 drew near I looked for evidence of activity on George's part which might indicate that a key of the door was being secretly fabricated by him. If he was not going to disappoint me he was certainly doing a good job of hiding any trace of his efforts.

Was I being foolishly naive or immature about the whole matter? No, damn it! I wasn't! I was proud of the fact that I had won my wings, seen action in air combat and acquitted myself adequately for a year as a prisoner before reaching the age of twenty-one. Today when I see twenty-one-year-old students, policemen or business men they seem mere babes, and yet here I was, a hard-bitten inmate of a prison, who had seen much and grown up very quickly. Surely I was entitled to some suitable recognition of my official coming of age!

As the days passed, and the eighth of October drew close, my mood alternated between a satisfied certainty that George would not let me down and an uneasy presentiment that he would dismiss the whole matter as a load of old rubbish not worthy of mature consideration. George was of the stuff by which the British army had achieved its reputation for steadfastness and unflinching devotion to duty. He was a rock, a man whom you could trust with your life: a man worthy of

Dixie Deans (in wheel chair) at RCAF ex-POW reunion in Oxford, England, 1982.

one's respect and friendship. But would he remember my birthday, and let me march proudly up to Dixie Deans to receive my symbolic recognition? "Damn you, George," I'd fume to myself, "you'd better come through or I'll never speak to you again." The next moment I would counter with "Come on, Ted, buck up and accept the fact that this is merely another day, and George is a friend in the ways that count most."

The morning of October 8 dawned no differently from any of the previous succession of identical days, which were beginning to blur into one another as I approached the first anniversary of life in captivity. George was no more and no less talkative than his usual stolid self. We drank a morning brew-up of coffee while we waited for nine o'clock parade, and exchanged the usual necessary observations concerning the day's events,

George Stamp on his wedding day, Stoke on Trent, England.

and planned for the preparation of the evening meal. There was no mention of, or reference to, any special sort of celebration.

Since it was George's day for preparing supper he would have ample opportunity to use our limited resources in any way he chose to prepare something different or special, if he elected to do so; but he gave no evidence of his plans, and I did not intend to drop any more hints. If he had not got the message by now, he never would.

The guards announced the morning parade with their usual assortment of whistles and gruff shouts of "Raus, raus fur appel." We slowly filed out and took up our customary positions in columns of fives to be counted. The camp *kommandant* observed the normal courtesies of German protocol, saluting smartly and appearing, as usual, impeccably groomed, and shod in gleaming black high boots. He clicked his heels as he returned the salute of his senior NCO, who announced that the count was correct, and the parade could be dismissed. There were no announcements by the German authorities this morning.

The *kommandant* indicated to Deans that the parade could be dismissed, saluted again and strode from the parade-ground. It was now the moment for the senior British NCO to make any announcements, or to simply dismiss the men. I waited for my big moment, mindful of the fact that I was very nervous, and acutely aware that my throat was so dry I'd be incapable of speaking.

With a simple "Parade is dismissed!" Dixie broke the tension which had built up in me. That was it! George's face was impassive, and bore no hint of an apologetic air as I searched his eyes for an explanation. There was still evening parade at six o'clock. Perhaps he had decided to leave it until then. I had to endure another nine hours of uncertainty. He had not even wished me a happy birthday! This was going to be a very long day indeed!

I don't recall much of the events of that day in the interval between morning and evening parade. I do remember thinking to myself that George would not be off the hook until the six o'clock count had been completed, and we had finished dinner later, which would be his last hurrah as far as I was concerned. I was beginning to feel like the young bride whose husband has failed to observe their first wedding anniversary.

When I look back now from a perspective of nearly fifty years the whole matter seems trivial. How could I have gotten so worked up over a birthday? It certainly was childish indeed. But then, many of the aspects of prisoner-of-war life were, I suppose, rather juvenile. Like everything else in life, these matters must be considered in light of the circumstances in which they occured.

As the day wore on and evening parade approached, I once again could feel my hopes rising. Once again the German guard detail entered the compound and summoned us to late-afternoon roll-call. Once more the formalities of counting the assembled men were completed. Hauptman Pfeifer stiffly saluted James Deans and turned the parade over to him, having satisfied himself that all were present and accounted for. I waited expectantly for my name to be called out, but again I was to be disappointed as Deans made some routine announcements and dismissed the parade. My moment of recognition was not to be. Perhaps George had decided to make a small private affair of it and would make a suitable comment over our evening meal. This was the final straw at which I grasped eagerly. After all, he was a man not given to a

Group of POWs at Stalag Luft III. Front row left to right Roger Rousseau, author, Don Sugden, unknown, Martin Platz, unknown. Rear row left to right Ivan Quinn, Bill Stephenson, unknown, Don Switzer, Bruce Robertson and Billy Sproule.

public display of personal feeling. He would quietly present my key to me and raise his mug of coffee to my good health in observance of my twenty-first. I would settle for that. It would not have the same sense of occasion as a public presentation, but at this point I was willing to settle for it.

We sat down to our daily meal which George had prepared. The usual German issue of boiled potatoes was ours to flesh out in any way we could, using the supplementary rations of Red Cross issue. I don't remember what we ate. We were always hungry for the one meal of any consequence, since breakfast and lunch were barely more than a slice of bread and possibly some soup at noon; but tonight the meal may as well have been sawdust. I had no stomach for the food which we ate in silence. If George guessed the reason for my lack of interest he never gave any indication of it. Since I have never been one to mask my feelings, I'm quite sure he sensed my unhappiness.

The subject was never raised again by me, and I never let him know how hurt I was. We continued messing together until the day that George's real identity was discovered by the German authorities and he was sent back to the British army prison camp.

Many years later I visited George in his home at Stoke on Trent. The man who greeted me was a shadow of the strong hard-bitten man I had remembered. George had survived a bout with tuberculosis and it had left its mark on him. His charming wife and lovely family, his neat and beautifully kept home were proof that he had made a successful transition to peacetime. George, old friend, if you ever read these words in print be assured that the recollections of those days we survived together are rich with memories of your strength and friendship: memories which more than counterbalance your one lapse from grace.

CHAPTER SEVEN
The Ice Rink

Brian came bounding into hut 57A with breathless haste, and glanced about to see how many fellow prisoners were dozing on their bunks, or reading quietly in the warm July afternoon. "You'll never guess what I've just heard!" he declared excitedly.

"The Russians have encircled the camp," volunteered a bored voice from the gloom of a bottom bunk.

"The invasion has begun?" was the hopeful response of another.

"All prisoners round the bend are to be repatriated."

"Come on fellows, be serious," said Brian. "Anyway if Jerry had agreed to repatriate all of unsound mind we'd all bloody well be going home on the next boat. Besides it's got nothing to do with the war. Do you want to hear my news or not?"

"Only if it's good," responded Dave, who was engaged in finding a red eight for his black seven from a grubby set of dog-eared playing cards spread out in the eternal game of solitaire displayed in front of him on the well-scrubbed table top.

"Of course it's good news," said Brian. "If it were bad, it wouldn't be news would it?"

The logic of that remark could not be disputed in July of 1943 when disaster after disaster had followed the fortunes of the Allies, and the news which filtered through German censors was slanted even further. Prisoners of war in German hands had become resigned to a long war, and any hopes of a return to England remained a very dim prospect.

"Are you ready for this?" continued Brian. "A Red Cross shipment of hockey equipment is sitting on the railway siding in the village, and Blackie says there are enough ice skates, hockey sticks, and goalie pads to equip two teams!" This triumphant announcement was accorded virtually no favourable reaction by his comrades.

"Big deal! What do we do with hockey equipment in July?"

"So what? Even if we are still here next winter what do we do for an ice rink? There isn't a square yard of ground suitable for building one, and unless you can commandeer a bulldozer from the goons, which is out of the question, there is no way you can level a piece of ground large enough, since we can't even put our hands on a spade or rake in the whole camp." This logical reply was reinforced by approving comments from most of the men.

As bad as the war news was, each prisoner could not admit, even to himself, the possibility of still another winter in enemy hands. To appear enthusiastic about Brian's news was an acknowledgement that one had given up hoping for some miracle of arms to turn the tide of warfare so that we would be home for Christmas. This was the *kriegie*'s perpetual bench-mark of hope. As one Christmas came and went the credo always remained the same: "Oh well, never mind, we are sure to be home for the next one." Boys who had been shot down in 1940 or 1941 and had already spent two or three

Christmases in captivity had more reasons than most of us to become discouraged at the prospect of experiencing another winter in German hands.

Brian, sensing that his news had awakened these trains of thought in his buddies, wisely let the matter drop. The routine of prison camp continued more or less undisturbed for a few days until I had the opportunity of raising the subject again with Dave.

We met one afternoon on the well-worn path which ran around the perimeter of the prison camp, just inside the warning wire. "Doing circuits" was the usual daily routine of nearly all prisoners as a means of taking exercise. Some chose to walk alone with their private thoughts, while most preferred a companion with whom they could conjecture and share hopes for the future. We walked in silence for some time. Then finally I broached the subject which had been on my mind for some time. I reminded Dave of what Brian had said about the hockey equipment.

Dave did not answer at first, and I didn't press him: he seldom said much without first thinking a lot. It was for this reason that I valued his opinion.

"I knew something was eating you," he finally replied. "Come on, out with it, what's on your mind?"

"Well I'm sure you're aware that among the Canadian flyers in this camp there are some pretty good hockey players from pre-war senior leagues. Bill used to play for the Sydney Millionaires, Perry played goal for the Cornwall Flyers. I'll bet we could put on quite a show for the English, Polish and Czech prisoners."

Dave began to warm to the subject. "We'd have to modify the rules to prohibit most of the bodily contact," he added, "because the equipment which arrived includes only sticks, skates, and pads for the goalkeeper."

"We could always improvise shin-pads and hockey gauntlets," I continued. "Let's talk to Vic Clarke about the chances of working on levelling a piece of ground for an ice rink. After all we have lots of spare time, and winter is quite a way off yet. If the rest of the fellows see us start, they might be willing to get involved."

Again Dave was silent for some time before replying. When he spoke again I knew I had picked the right man with whom to discuss the pros and cons of the project.

"I think I'd like to work with you on this project, Ted," was his response. "You know its going to be a monumental task shifting all that dirt around if we have to rely on just the two of us with a couple of spades. Do you think Jerry will even allow it? You know how suspicious he'll become if he sees dirt being moved around." This was a reference, of course, to the never-ending tunnelling which was going on in prison camps all over Germany, and against which the German authorities were obliged to take ever more forceful action, including even the use of seismographic equipment.

"You know, there is one other thing we haven't considered," I said. "This extra effort is going to burn up a lot of calories. We're going to be hungry all the time."

"I thought of that," said Dave with a slight shrug. He turned and smiled rather ruefully. "I'm still game if you are."

So it was decided, and a day or so later after morning parade, I was able to bring the matter up with Vic Clarke, the senior

Group of Canadian POWs prepare for the game of hockey in Stalag Luft I.

NCO. If anyone could get Jerry's co-operation it was Vic, a British flyer who had the respect of all prisoners and Germans alike for his gentlemanly manner combined with a fearless and stubborn attitude in all matters related to the welfare of his men. "After all," he remarked, "since Jerry has allowed the hockey equipment into the camp he can't very well deny us the chance to at least build a suitable hockey pitch."

"That's hockey *rink*, not pitch," I corrected. Vic laughed. "Whatever you say. What equipment will you need? Remember, I can't promise anything, but I'll do my best."

"Fair enough," I replied. "We'll settle for half a dozen shovels and a couple of rakes."

A week later Clarke asked me to drop around to his office after morning *appel*. Because of his position as spokesman for all Allied NCOs in the camp, he was entitled to the privilege of a more-or-less private room, which consisted of a small sort of guardhouse built onto the end of hut 52, with space for two double bunks, and a small table in the centre of the room. In the corner stood a small woodstove which served to warm food and to take the chill off the living quarters in the winter months. He shared this luxury with three others.

"Jerry has agreed to let you have half a dozen spades and a couple of rakes. His only stipulation is that they always remain visible during the day, and be returned to the main gate every evening, which is fair enough I believe, don't you?"

I was more than satisfied and thanked Vic for his efforts. "There is one other thing," added Vic. "You will understand that the present playing-field cannot be used. It is in constant use for rugger, soccer, softball et cetera. You will have to find somewhere to build your ice rink without disturbing the existing sports facilities. Morale is most important and our games programs cannot be interfered with."

"That's no problem. I plan on building the rink between huts 57A and 58A. All we will be disturbing will be a few clothes-lines. The rink will be narrower than regulation, but its not a major problem. In fact a full-sized rink would be a bit much for us to handle, given our general lack of conditioning. Thanks again, Vic, for your efforts on our behalf."

"Thank *you*," replied the senior N.C.O. Anything which kept his restless charges occupied and interested contributed to morale and helped lighten his sometimes-heavy load.

We commenced work the next day. At first a few fellow prisoners complained about raising dust on the laundry hanging out, but a few drops of water sprinkled on the work area eased that problem. The work schedule provided for an hour in the morning and an hour in the late afternoon which by the end of the first day was more than enough as we surveyed the blisters on the palms of our softened hands. By the end of the first week we had settled into a fairly steady routine of monotonously transferring earth from the high spots to the lower areas. It became evident very soon that the camp had been built on fill dumped on top of glacial debris consisting of large and small boulders. The larger boulders had to be somehow moved or broken up. Lacking sledge hammers and wheelbarrows, the only solution in some cases was to dig under them and let them fall under their own weight further into the soil. It was discouraging work. An entire week was expended on one such rock which eventually sunk obstinately out of sight. Some of the rocks which at first appeared to be quite small were like icebergs, with most of their bulk hidden below the surface, and the work was slowed so much as a consequence that by the end of August there was not much to show for our labours.

There was, however, one fortunate consequence of the growing pile of stones which accumulated from our efforts, and strangely enough it came from the Germans themselves in the form of packets of flower seeds. The rocks were ideal for building ornamental rock gardens; there was plenty of soil and water and there was compost material readily available from tea-leaves, coffee-grounds, potato peelings and other food waste. Before long some quite attractive and colourful gardens had sprouted up. It was excellent therapy for the English prisoners who were nearly all born gardeners, and it did wonders to brighten up the drab and dreary aspect of the camp. It had one other consequence of a more practical nature as well. Some of the gardeners began to volunteer their assistance, which we were pleased to accept, and by mid-October it began to look as though the bulk of the work was behind us, and we would be able to relax our efforts somewhat. Nature, too, lent assistance in the form of early autumn rainfalls, which helped to point out uneven spots in the gradually emerging ice rink. By the time the colder winds of early winter began to blow the only work remaining to be done was a final levelling off with the use of large planks through which nails had been driven. When these improvised tools were dragged across the surface of the ground they very efficiently dragged soil from high areas and deposited it in the hollows. Now indeed we had a suitable surface which awaited its first flooding.

One of the principal differences between a pleasure skating rink and a hockey cushion is the boarding which encloses the playing area. Much of the action in the game of ice hockey takes place along the boards. There was no chance of persuading Jerry to supply sufficient lumber, but there was no reason why a makeshift enclosure could not be accomplished using a mixture of snow, earth and water which, when allowed to freeze, would serve quite well. It would only be a foot or so high, but would certainly be better than nothing. Suitable goalie nets would have to be made, but these could be easily fabricated using a minimum supply of wood. As to the actual netting material, old and worn-out sweaters were unravelled and the yarn twisted into strands strong enough to make two quite professional-looking goals.

"It looks like you two fellows have pulled it off after all." The comment was made by Blackie White on a frosty December morning. Blackie was the unofficial sports director for Canadian POWs in the camp. He had been an outstanding all-round athlete in pre-war days, and had combined these talents with his enthusiastic interest and his concern for his fellow prisoners' welfare in all things concerning fitness and athletics. Together with his British and other Allied flyer counterparts, he had succeeded in organizing well-run soccer, basketball, softball, rugger and cricket matches. Thanks to their efforts there was no reason for any prisoner of war to complain of there being nothing to do if he possessed any athletic ability at all. All of these sporting activities were well run at various levels of competence so that there was no reason for anyone to feel excluded.

"Now that it looks like we're going to have ice," I responded, "we were wondering if you would get everyone interested together so that we could get a feeling for how the fellows would like to organize the games. Then we could draw up some rules, pick up teams, and schedule some actual games."

"I'd be glad to," replied Blackie. "I hope you don't feel as though I'm muscling in. I'm the first to admit that we didn't actually think you'd be able to do it, and we haven't been all that helpful these past few months."

"That's okay, we enjoyed the work. There is one suggestion we'd like to make though," I added. "Since most of the English, Polish and Czech prisoners are not familiar with Canada's national game, we thought it would be rather exciting to put on a real show before we get down to regular league play. So why not pick up two scratch teams from our twenty or so absolute-best players and put on an exhibition match?"

"I'll get cracking on it right away," promised Blackie. "Let's hope the weather co-operates." This last remark was prophetic in light of what was to happen.

Just after Christmas of 1943 the weather in East Prussia turned cold and by New Year's Day several inches of snow lay on the ground. It was time to commence building an ice surface! Using any containers capable of holding liquid the long task of moving water from the wash-house to the ice rink began. The most efficient method was a modified type of bucket brigade, whereby containers of water were passed hand to hand along a long line of volunteers, until the end of the line was reached. Saucepans, billycans, Klim tins, some few buckets with handles, kettles, jugs, night latrine pails, coffee-pots, bowls, cans, bottles and canisters were passed to the awaiting "flooder" who carefully selected the most logical spot to dump the precious water. Slowly the ice rink took shape. If only the cold weather held we would have our rink in a day or so. We practically willed the sun to stay hidden so that our precious ice would not be melted away. Low areas received special attention. A mixture of snow and water was packed down to achieve a satisfactory base for further watering. There were now no bare areas. The entire surface was covered with a layer of ice - not very thick, but enough to warrant a preliminary test skate. Dave and I picked out skates, laced them on and skated happily around for some few moments, finally pronouncing the hockey cushion ready for play.

By this time a great deal of interest had been generated for the project, and when Blackie announced that an exhibition hockey match was to take place the following day, there was scarcely a prisoner in the entire camp who was not looking forward to the game, scheduled for two o'clock in the afternoon. Canada's reputation as the originator of the game of ice hockey had been justly earned and gloriously maintained by such revered names as Howie Morenz, Lionel Conacher, Cyclone Taylor, Georges Vezina, and such combinations as the famous kid line of the Toronto Maple Leafs of Joe Primeau, Harvey "Busher" Jackson, and Charlie Conacher. Who could forget the famous S line of the Montreal Maroons consisting of Nels Stewart, Babe Siebert, and Hooley Smith, and other illustrious names who had filled the adolescent hearts of young Canadians with hero-worship. The memories of their exploits had been carried into the furthest reaches of Nazi Germany in the minds of the now-languishing prisoners. And now in the

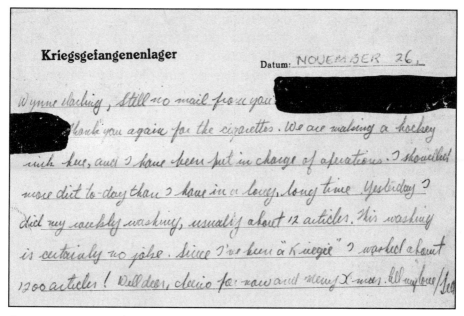

Kriegsgefangenenlager   Datum: NOVEMBER 26,

Wynne darling, Still no mail from you ▮▮▮▮▮ Thank you again for the cigarettes. We are making a hockey rink here, and I have been put in charge of operations. I shovelled more dirt to-day than I have in a long, long time. Yesterday I did my weekly washing, usually about 12 articles. This washing is certainly no joke. Since I've been a "Kriegie" I washed about 1200 articles! Well dear, cheerio for now and merry X-mas. All my love / Jack

Censored postcard to fiancée from East Prussia. Missing words were "since moving to this camp."

heart of this foreign land, it was finally going to happen: the next afternoon, twenty Canadian hockey players would give a demonstration of their national game.

The following day was crisp, cold and sunny. The ice had been newly flooded. It shimmered and sparkled in the morning sun like a lake of frozen diamonds. It seemed almost a profane act to mar its perfection with the cutting action of twelve pairs of skates which would soon be zipping up and down on its unblemished surface. As game time neared, the more avid fans began to take up strategic locations around the rink and on the roof-tops of the barracks between which the game was to be played. For the time being the war was forgotten as a feeling of excitement and anticipation mounted in each Canadian's heart, matched by similar feelings of interest and curiosity among the British and European prisoners. As the players stepped on the ice surface for the ritualistic pre-game warm-up skate, shouts of "Way to go Canada! Up the colonies!" and other friendly banter commenced to echo back and forth. Then the puck was dropped and play commenced.

The Canadian players did not disappoint anyone. For a blissful hour the prisoners were treated to an exhibition of clean, fast action, dexterity and skill, which even the least knowledgeable could not fail to appreciate. Never mind that two or three end-to-end rushes produced near exhaustion in the undernourished participants. A brief rest while being spelled off by other eager replacements and the sheer euphoria of the contest aided by a few heaving gulps of fresh air drawn into gasping lungs rejuvenated the athletes. Never mind the score! Each goal was applauded for its artistry alone as the puck was thrown from stick blade to stick blade with crisp and accurate skill, culminating in a bullet-like shot on goal, resulting in a brilliant save or an electrifying score. It was fast and exciting, exhilarating and spectacular, and by game's end the drained and exhausted players stood shakily to acknowledge the cheers and acclaim of all. It had been a day to remember: a sample of what would come in the days ahead as other eager skaters took to the ice to match skills.

But it was not to be. The sun went down that evening swollen into a glorious fire-ball magnified by ice crystals held in the high cirrus clouds, portending the approach of a warm front and an accompanying storm. All night the rain pounded on the roofs of the barracks. In the morning the ice rink was a miniature lake, spilling through the weakened makeshift barrier that contained it. Our rink was gone, and with it all our hopes for relief from the soul-destroying boredom of another winter in Germany.

The cold weather stayed away. It meant much to the morale of German armies and civilians, that winter of 1943/44, but it did little for the feelings of the Canadian prisoners of war who gazed longingly at the almost-new hockey equipment. Except for that brief afternoon of supremely enjoyable competition, it remained unused for the balance of the winter.

Dave's only comment when asked about the months of effort and back-breaking work was a smile, a shrug and a brief "C'est la guerre!"

CHAPTER EIGHT
The Wager

It began innocently enough. A simple argument over the gastronomic capacity of the airmen of the Royal Air Force from the north of England versus the rest. "The rest" included all of the remainder of the British Isles, the Commonwealth, and Allied airmen from all over Europe and the United States. It was no small and idle boast that Johnny Coates from Newcastle upon Tyne was making. He was a stocky man, inclined to be belligerent in all matters which touched upon the masculinity and virility of him and his fellow Tyne-siders. "We can drink anyone here under the table, anywhere, anytime, and choose your own booze," he roared to his amused comrades. There was little chance of his ever having to prove this statement in a prisoner-of-war camp where the sole alcoholic binge was a once-a-year Bacchanalia at Christmas time on half a litre per man of watered German beer.

"When it comes to eating and drinking, nobody can keep up with an honest working man from Newcastle at dinner time," Johnny boasted.

"If that's true, I'm glad I'm not in your combine," remarked one of the group who were gathered for the usual morning natter, a daily ritual whereby the breakfast period was extended and events of the day discussed. Since breakfast usually consisted of a single slice of German black bread which was three parts sawdust and one part whole grain, the illusion of a full meal was difficult to achieve. The prisoners sipped the morning brew of tea made from a third or fourth distillation of carefully dried tea-leaves from a British Red Cross parcel. It was somehow unthinkable to throw away tea-leaves after a single brew. Many a Canadian prisoner was to discover the marvellously rejuvenating qualities of the traditional English mug of tea. It provided a momentary escape from the dreary realities of a spartan existence. Under its comforting influence one laid aside, for a few brief moments, the sense of frustration as the dramatic events of a world in conflict passed one by.

A combine could consist of two men or as many as twenty, or even more. In theory, of course, all prisoners ate the same grub. But somehow, larger combines appeared to stretch the meagre rations further, particularly when the Red Cross parcels were getting through, and the rare treats and tidbits they contained were lumped together. In Stalag Luft III near Sagan in the summer of 1942, to paraphrase Charles Dickens' words, it was the best of the worst of times. Life in a German prisoner-of-war camp was without doubt the worst of times for flyers who, although they had been risking their lives daily in their dangerous profession, were at least used to eating and drinking well in the messes of English bomber stations. These bad times were, however, alleviated by regular issue of Red Cross parcels which had now been well-organized, and were arriving with gratifying regularity. It is safe to say that all ex-prisoners of war, when recalling their POW days, will remember with affection and appreciation the Red Cross, and all who were connected with, and responsible for their efforts. For a short period during this summer of 1942 Red Cross parcels did arrive weekly. When the war began to go badly for Germany they became more infrequent, and for long periods ceased completely. For these reasons that summer was decidedly the best of the worst of times.

Sergeant Johnny Coates was not a man given to idle boasts. If he made a statement he was always ready to back it up with action. As the discussion became more heated he decided that if a challenge was to be made he was the man to make it. It was time to show these fellows that he was prepared to defend his honour with appropriate action. He stood up and signalled for silence.

"I would be willing to wager the contents of a Red Cross parcel that I, Johnny Coates, in the period between sunrise and sunset can eat, and keep down, the contents of said Red Cross parcel. If I lose, which I won't, I will give my next parcel issue to whoever accepts this challenge!" There was a paralysing silence following this declaration, finally broken by Arthur Ault who was one of three others who messed together with Johnny.

"Hold it, Johnny! That's our grub you're talking about, too, you know."

"I'm aware of that and I'm willing to temporarily suspend our combine arrangements for as long as it takes to settle this, but if I win, we stand to gain an extra parcel issue which I'm willing to share equally with you three."

Arthur was obviously impressed with Johnny's sincerity and willingness to go it alone if necessary. He spoke to Taffy Evans and George Lambert who had, up to now, remained silent, but who had been listening with amused expressions on their face. Taffy and George were the other two members of Johnny's combine. "What do you two think?" he asked.

"Oh hell, let's give it a bash. What have we got to lose except a little belt tightening," was George's contribution.

"What about you Taffy?" asked Arthur.

"If Johnny loses, we stand to lose two Red Cross parcels, not one. The one he attempts to eat and the one being wagered, but what the heck! I say let him try. Anything for a bit of fun."

"Well that settles that," said Johnny, very pleased with his friends' support. "Now all we need is someone to take me on."

Yank Howard was a quiet-spoken American who had enlisted in the Royal Canadian Air Force prior to the entry of the United States into the conflict. He was much respected by all for his friendliness and for his obvious willingness to keep his opinions regarding American participation in the conflict to himself. He was the very opposite of what most Englishmen envisioned as the loud-mouthed, opinionated, American bull-shooter. He was somewhat of an individualist, preferring to go it alone as far as messing arrangements were concerned. His usual rejoinder when asked about his preference was, "I haven't enough will-power to ration my grub, so I like to feel if I want to I can live high on the hog on parcel-issue day, and not have to account to anyone else if I decide to eat a whole tin of corned beef at once, or wolf down a quarter-pound of chocolate in one glorious binge." He saw in Johnny Coates a bit of a kindred spirit and his competitive instincts decided the matter for him.

"I'll tell you what, Johnny," he volunteered quietly. "Not only will I accept your challenge, but I'll make a few concessions since I'm not prepared to see you commit suicide by eating an entire one pound tin of Canadian butter in one day, not to mention a bar of castile soap. I presume we are talking about

Canadian Red Cross parcels rather than English parcels since they're the ones which are currently being received in this camp."

"Okay Yank, it's a bet," responded Johnny and he extended his hand to his American challenger. "Since you're making a concession, so will I. If I lose, which I won't, I will go on Jerry rations for as long as it takes to pay back my combine."

"That won't be necessary, Johnny," said Arthur, Taffy and George in unison, "although we appreciate the offer."

A word of explanation is necessary here in order to understand what the bet entailed. What follows is a list of the contents from Canadian and British food parcels.

Canadian

1 tin powdered milk (454g)
1 can of butter (454g)
1 tin of corned beef (454g)
1 tin of bacon (454g)
1 bar of cheese
1 tin of salmon
1 tin sardines
1 box of raisins (454g)
1 jar of jam (340g)
1 box 12 large soda biscuits
1 bar of chocolate (600g)
1 tin instant coffee
salt & pepper
1 bar of soap
sugar (230g)

British

1 tin of condensed milk
1 tin of corned beef (454g)
1 tin of spam (454g)
1 tin of lemon curd
1 bar of chocolate (340g)
tea (230g)
8 marmite cubes
1 tin of kippers in sauce
1 tin of jam (280g)
1 tin curry powder
margarine (230g)
1 tin 50 cigarettes
1 bar soap
sugar (170g)

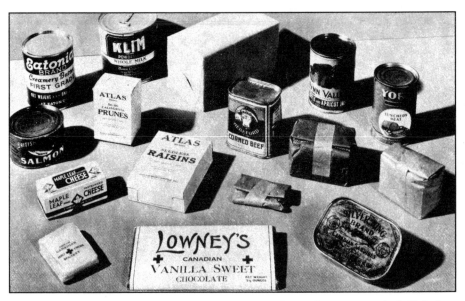

Contents of a typical Canadian Red Cross food package. Contents varied slightly.

And so it was agreed. The challenge had been made and accepted, and duly witnessed by all. The attempt was to be made the following Tuesday commencing at sunrise - which would be approximately 5 am in the long spring days of late May - and was to be won or lost by sunset, around 9 pm. Tuesday was chosen because it followed parcel-issue day, which was every Monday.

Tremendous interest was generated instantly throughout the entire camp. It was unheard of for someone to risk a week's food ration on a gamble of this nature. True, German rations were not involved. If he lost he could fall back on them. But the prospect of existing on these alone was not pleasant to the long-term prisoner who had survived a year of German rations. A bowl of watery soup, four or five small potatoes, a slab of black bread and ersatz coffee or mint tea was the daily issue from the German kitchen. It was a guarantee for permanent hunger pains, and led to remarks such as "Some

92

bloody fool is going to risk his parcel issue by wagering its contents that he can down it in one day! He must be nuts!" Others were visibly impressed by Johnny's adventurous spirit and his willingness to undertake such an extraordinary feat. The betting was fairly evenly divided. Anyone desiring to lay down twenty Players on Johnny's ability to pull it off found a willing taker, and, conversely, a prisoner who was convinced that it could not be done was asked to back up his conviction with a suitable wager. As Tuesday approached Johnny was seen to be constantly engaged in building up his appetite and using up his calorie reserves by walking endless circuits around the exercise path. One thing was certain: when the sun rose Tuesday morning he would be as ravenous as a wolf! As he plodded valiantly and endlessly around the circuit he was constantly approached by enthusiastic supporters offering advice, and by others who were convinced that his chances of accomplishing the feat were negligible. With all of them Johnny kept his cool and responded amiably enough, preferring to let his gastronomic capacity speak for him.

The messing arrangements in prison camps did not lend themselves to such spectator sports as watching eating competitions. Bunks were arranged in such a way so as to permit each combine to eat in relative privacy. A table which would permit six or eight men to mess together was usually obstructed from the view of others by triple-decked bunks, and only if the barrack's wooden shutters were opened could any person observe mealtime activities. The large amount of interest in Johnny Coates' challenge therefore had to be satisfied by second-hand reports of the few fortunate men able to gather near the opened shutters near his mess table. He was not a particularly shy or reclusive person, and had no objection to being the centre of attention whilst dining. His only stipulation was that spectators not completely block the flow of fresh air.

Some wag suggested that his table be moved to the middle of the football pitch and an admission of two cigarettes be charged for spectators. This was rejected as being impractical, although Johnny, I am quite sure, would have agreed to it.

One of the stipulations that Johnny and Yank had agreed to was that the bet would be postponed if the Monday parcel issue were to be cut back. An issue of less than one per man would have resulted in Johnny's messing buddies, Arthur, Taffy and George, being further deprived if a complete parcel was to be supplied for the attempt. Fortunately this situation did not materialize. At this stage of the war transportation was still fairly reliable in Germany, and stocks of Red Cross parcels remained quite high. When Monday arrived and each prisoner was issued with a full parcel the bet was declared officially on.

When the evening roll-call was completed, and prisoners were locked in the huts for the night, everyone settled down to the various activities by which the long hours were somehow passed until lights out. Card games were the most popular pastime. Reading was a close second. Any good book or recent best seller which arrived in camp via the Red Cross or in a personal package from home soon contained on its flyleaf a long list of names of prisoners waiting to read it. The books passed quickly from man to man since the long hours of inactivity made the turnover very rapid. Some of the men studied languages or accountancy, or lay on their bunks and day-dreamed of the day when the war would be over. Others engaged in noisy arguments over the conduct of the war, or politics or religion. The latter subjects were dangerous and the participants were very quickly requested to "put a sock in it" when it showed signs of becoming too violent. As the hut went into darkness at 11 pm it was the usual custom, by common agreement, to listen to records on a wind-up record player for a half-hour or so. The music did indeed assist those with particular personal problems to cast them off for a short period, and to bring sleep and a few hours of blessed oblivion to the camp-weary, restless, and desperately homesick men. As the record player was shut down that evening and quietness descended on the hut someone remarked quietly, "At least by this time tomorrow one of us will go to bed with a full stomach." There was a murmur of agreement from all.

The following morning at 5 am Johnny Coates was up and about as were his combine partners Arthur, Taffy and George. His strategy was quite simple. He would commence eating and drinking at the agreed time and continue to do so with suitable exercise breaks until the deadline of 9 pm. His pre-breakfast snack consisted of a "Canadian biscuit," as the heavy crackers in the Red Cross parcel were called, of which there were twelve in all. Each cracker, when soaked in milk or water, usually swelled to such a size that it covered the entire bottom of an average-sized frying pan. Demolishing a dozen of these crackers alone was no mean feat. To wash it down he drank three cups of instant coffee with thickly mixed powdered milk to which a couple of generous spoonfuls of sugar had been added. Arthur suggested to him that perhaps he should spread some of the jam on the large cracker to "help it go down." "Good idea," agreed Johnny.

By the time the rest of the one hundred and sixty or so men of the hut were up and stirring about, Johnny was preparing for a pre-breakfast exercise stroll and a morning wash, and when the guards opened the barrack doors to start a new day at 6 am he was first man out. Morning parade was at 8 am. He had decided to walk steadily until 7 am, at which time he would sit down to his breakfast and attempt to put away most of the bacon with a slab of fried Canadian biscuit to help absorb its high fat content. He instructed George to fry it crisp and drain off most of the fat. While George was engaged in preparing

Johnny's huge breakfast many pairs of eyes watched in wonder and amazement. To actually witness an entire week's ration of bacon in the pan at once was an incredible luxury, and the tantalizing aroma it gave off to the rest of the hut was, to say the least, unnerving.

Promptly at 7 am Johnny sat down to breakfast. The hut doors had been opened at 6 am, so the outside of the open window near his dining area had been long since crowded with ringsiders eager to enjoy the spectacle. The bunks which surrounded the table where he sat eating were crowded as well, and the comments from the interested watchers were mostly encouraging.

By parade time the bacon was gone as well as two more cups of coffee and a dry Canadian biscuit thickly spread with jam. As the German guards entered the hut and ordered "Raus, raus, fur appel," Johnny responded with a satisfied burp and a contented sigh. "That should hold me until mid-morning brew up."

Mid-morning "brew up" or "elevenses" was a daily ritual which served to break up the period between morning parade and the lunch period. It was largely a social affair. Tea or coffee and conversation flowed in equal proportions. Today for Johnny Coates it was his third meal of the day. He had decided to tackle a tin of sardines with the inevitable Canadian biscuit and a couple of cups of coffee. He was permitted to enjoy this snack in relative peace since most of the men rarely missed the mid-morning opportunity to discuss items of current interest. He polished off the sardines with apparent enjoyment and wasted no time in joining the walkers in order to burn off as many calories as possible before lunch. He would attempt then to put away half of the corned beef. If he could do that and keep it down he reasoned that his chances would be excellent of winning his bet. He had by now finished four of the Canadian soda biscuits, and eight more remained.

At one o'clock he commenced eating again. Those of you who have eaten tinned corned beef need not be reminded how hearty and satisfying a meal a relatively thin slice can be. Johnny's task was to eat for lunch half a tin plus two more biscuits. He did so, but was obviously toying with the last few scraps and finding the dry biscuits more and more difficult to swallow. The coffee helped, but it was heavily sugared and the level of powdered milk in the half-kilo tin had not dropped as much as his now rather concerned friends had hoped.

He had the afternoon to work on the raisins and chocolate. Faced with this, his chances of being hungry and ready for his evening meal did not appear too rosy, but he was confident of his ability to accomplish the feat, and greeted all his well-wishers with a grand show of confidence as he plodded grimly all of that long afternoon in circuit after circuit of the perimeter track around the camp. By evening parade he had succeeded in finishing off the chocolate and the raisins and even managed a half-hearted attempt at a show of eager anticipation for his next onslaught on the food which still remained.

A brief recapitulation is in order at this point. With a break for coffee at mid-afternoon he had, by the time parade was over at 5:30 pm, eaten and managed to keep down half of the powdered milk, half of the corned beef, one pound of bacon, one tin of sardines, a box of raisins, approximately four ounces of the jam, half of the soda biscuits, a large bar of chocolate, half of the instant coffee and four ounces of sugar.

He still had a tin of salmon as well as the remainder of the corned beef, six ounces of cheese, eight ounces of jam, the rest of the coffee, sugar, and powdered milk and those bloody Canadian biscuits which were by now lying very heavily in his gut. Johnny had not made provision for one important thing in his previous proud boast. After nearly two years in captivity existing on short rations, his stomach had shrunk, as had the stomachs of all his comrades. The human body adapts to changed circumstances, and the months of deprivation had in various degrees made it possible for the prisoners to satisfy their appetites with a relatively small intake of food.

Nevertheless, at six o'clock he sat down to his evening meal. The tin of salmon was the best Pacific brand, and he was able to make fairly short work of it. He then turned bravely to the corned beef which appeared by now to his eyes to fairly drip with greasy fat. It required a huge effort of will to make the stodgy stuff go down. Slowly and with grim determination he continued to eat and drink. Two more glutinous crackers disappeared and four only remained. "Have some cheese," suggested Arthur. "Perhaps a spot of cheese and crackers would make a little change." Johnny responded with a bilious smile. "Thanks, Arthur, I'll settle for some fresh air," he replied, and walked rather quickly to the hut door. Taffy and George exchanged glances and rose hastily to follow him.

For the next half-hour or so the three men plodded in silence around the camp. The only sound was an occasional long and gassy belch. Johnny's face had lost its normal ruddy hue. A greyish pallor lay on his cheeks and the whites of his eyes appeared to be slightly yellow. "Try some deep breathing," urged George as Johnny fought a compulsive urge to throw up. The muscles of his distended gut expanded and contracted as the waves of gas forced themselves through his lower intestine and his digestive system did what it had to do to achieve relief. The awe-inspiring rumbles, belches, burps and farts were heart-rending to his concerned buddies. In any other circumstances it would have been most indelicate to say the least. To Taffy and George it was merely an indication that Johnny's ordeal would soon be over, one way or another. He was a determined man, however, and at eight o'clock, with one hour to go before the agreed deadline, he valiantly made his final onslaught on the food in a do-or-die effort to justify his name and reputation. He lifted a cracker thickly covered with rich cheese to his face and attempted to chew. As he did so, a powerful wave of nausea hit him without warning. He struggled to control it and felt it gradually subside. He tried a sip of the hot, thickly creamed and heavily sweetened coffee and obtained a temporary measure of relief. Once again he shut his eyes and bit into the cheese and cracker. Again the violent nausea gripped him and he staggered wildly to the door heaving and emitting frightful wretching noises. He made it that far but no further. As his comrades watched in sympathetic awe and wonderment, Johnny tossed his cookies. Wave after wave hit him with a relentless authority which he was powerless to control. His only conscious desire now was to get relief as soon as possible from the terrible gut-wrenching spasms which tore at him. Gradually the violent, shuddering convulsions grew weaker, and finally subsided sufficiently to permit a weak grin to appear on Johnny's greyish face to which a little colour was now returning.

"Where's Yank?" he asked weakly. "He's not here, Johnny," replied George. "I guess I owe him a Red Cross parcel, but frankly I don't care just now whether I see one again for some time," he grinned. Yank was too much of a gentleman to be in at the kill and had tactfully refrained from witnessing Johnny's final moment of truth. When he was informed that he had won his wager he merely smiled and indicated that it was not his intention to hold him to it. If the incident had provided some degree of entertainment, and had given the fellows something to talk about for a few days, that was enough; to which the generally agreed response by all was "Jolly good show!"

This should have seen the end of the affair, but one final event occured the following day which serves to bring the entire episode into proper perspective. If there was a moral to be learned it was eloquently pointed out by Dixie Deans, the camp leader, the following morning on parade.

As the German *kommandant* dismissed the men at roll-call the next morning Dixie saluted him and turned to the assembled parade. "Before you go gentlemen, I have something to say. May I have your attention please?" The men were silent. George turned to Taffy and Arthur and whispered, "Oh, oh! I can guess what's coming."

"Gentlemen, it has come to my attention that some stupid idiot attempted yesterday, on a wager, to consume an entire Red Cross food parcel at once. While I cannot control what you do with this food which is issued to you to supplement German rations, and once issued is yours to consume as you wish, may I point out something which should be obvious to all of you. A large number of people have spent a great deal of time, money and effort to ensure a flow of these packages through a war-torn country to reach this camp. Valuable shipping space and railway lines which are hopelessly overloaded have been alloted by German authorities to ensure their safe transit. German rations are admittedly low, and we rely on these parcels to ease the hardships, but you can rest assured that if they become aware of the frivolous manner in which some of us treat them they will very quickly decide they are not a high enough priority item to justify the effort. Indeed, lives have been risked, since you are surely aware that anything that moves in Germany is a prime target for Allied air attacks. The International Red Cross headquarters in

Geneva would be justifiably furious should they become aware that their efforts on your behalf have been so lightly thought of. I shall not further embarrass the thoughtless person by naming him. I understand most, if not all of you already know who he is. It should be punishment enough to let him reflect on his own stupidity. That is all gentlemen. Parade is dismissed."

Johnny Coates was suitably chastened by these remarks, as he should have been. It was a dumb thing to do, and he was genuinely sorry for making such an ass of himself. Even so there were some who remained of the opinion it had been worth it, but they kept it to themselves. Far from being snubbed or sneered at, he had gained a measure of notoriety which revealed itself for some time in the friendly jibes and remarks of his friends who, in spite of it all, entertained a certain amount of reluctant admiration for his valiant attempt and his willingness to back up his words with action.

CHAPTER NINE
Baa Baa Black Sheep

One of the principal requirements of prisoner-of-war life was the ability to "dummy the count"; that is, to lead German captors to believe that they had custody of more prisoners than they actually had. Escaped prisoners naturally required all the assistance that could be given them, and if Jerry could be kept unaware of missing prisoners for a few days, the head start obtained could increase the chance of a successful "home run." Buried deep within Germany, and surrounded by occupied Europe as we were, the chances of actually making it to a neutral country or to England were astronomically against; but escaped Allied comrades were owed this much, at least, and roll-calls became a twice-daily battle of wits between prisoners and captors.

Roll-calls were frequently of long duration. Although intended to be orderly parades, they frequently deteriorated into sergeant majors' nightmares, as frustrated Germans attempted to reconcile the counts. Discrepancies were often, of course, the result of errors, and these errors were occasionally justifiable, since simple head counts were not usually practical nor indeed simple. In a prisoner-of-war camp of two thousand Allied flyers, the population was never stable. New arrivals, transfers to and from camp hospital, prisoners excused parade for various reasons, deaths, transfers to other camps, escapees, all contributed to the difficulties encountered by the *kommandant* and his staff. Add to this the fact that the guards were frequently those excused from active military service in a country desperate for manpower, and consequently were not always very bright, and it becomes quite remarkable that the count ever agreed with anything. The *kommandant*, however, was the man responsible, the man under the gun so to speak, the man who carried the unenviable load of accounting for his unruly flock. To have to account to higher authorities for missing men was his ultimate dread. It could result in his being relieved of his command and transferred to active service on the Eastern Front. He indeed required a high degree of co-operation from prisoners to achieve the accurate twice-daily roll-call. This co-operation was never forthcoming. The opposite was always the case. There were many ways open to falsify the count, and all of them were used. Frequently the perplexed guards attempted to fathom an apparent excess of Allied bodies on the morning parade, which by evening roll had shrunk to a shortage. The long roll-calls which resulted were not pleasant experiences, particularly in the cold of winter. The prisoners had time, and lots of it, but since the guards were longing to get it over and retire to the local beer halls, the resultant frustrations could sometimes produce potentially ugly incidents.

Some of the methods used to inflate the head count were quite innovative. Sergeant Prune, our lifelike dummy, was frequently pressed into service. His arms, being made of wood, made it very easy for his two buddies to hold him up while German guards performed the twice-daily chore of counting heads. If they had looked more closely they would have noticed that he was rather stiff-jointed and tended to collapse if not firmly supported. Since weird headgear was the norm rather than the exception among prisoners, the guards were not unduly suspicious of strange characters with balaclava hats which covered most of their faces. In the warm weather even the most bored guard might get somewhat curious upon seeing a *kriegie* wearing a greatcoat and elaborate head covering, so it was necessary to give Sergeant Prune some character, with an attempt at some sort of features. Even then the guards could not have looked too closely, since it is on record that as an experiment in testing the powers of observation of the average German soldier, Sergeant Prune appeared on parade with his head on backwards and was duly counted. Whether this reflects on the mentality of the wardens or attests to the somewhat vacant expression of the average Allied prisoner of war on *appel* has never been resolved.

Sergeant Prune could also remain in bed to be counted, since prisoners of war too sick to attend roll-call, but not ill enough to be in sick-bay, were excused parade and were counted separately. Most often a sympathetic German guard could be encouraged not to look too closely at a recumbent figure in bed, especially when a cigarette or two was offered as a friendly bribe, along with a quiet request not to waken old Ginger who was feeling very poorly this morning. Another method, quite a bit more risky of course, was to have the ill prisoner, once counted, suddenly recover and with a little fancy footwork appear on parade. This required perfect timing and an element of luck. The volunteer for this caper frequently ended up in the cooler for twenty-one days.

Multiple escapes of groups of prisoners at one time were more difficult to cover for, but not impossible. Remember, Jerry was trying to reconcile a head count which was made up of many parts of a whole: those on parade, those ill in bed or in sick-bay, those recently departed to other camps, together with guests in the cooler, essential cook house personnel, burial parties, newly arrived prisoners and temporary working parties engaged in unloading Red Cross parcels. Each of these separate groups provided opportunities for cooking the books, limited only by the boundless abilities of scheming minds to add or subtract bodies. Also, since the German army soldier always counted in *funf*s, or fives, if a particular party of men contained three or four left-overs it was frequently beyond their abilities to produce two counts in a row which agreed. The advantage was in our favour and it was used to the utmost.

As the war progressed it became an ever-increasing battle of wits between opposing sides, each to counteract the measures taken by the other. We were compelled by the need to cover for escapees, and the Germans were determined to round up Allied airmen roaming around the country before the heavy hand of the Gestapo was drawn into the conflict. When the Gestapo, pulled from other pressing duties, became involved it suggested that the German army was incapable of maintaining order and control over its charges, and their methods used to re-establish control were both brutal and efficient. As unpleasant as it was for prisoners to be subjected to Gestapo counts and searches, it was without question more so for the embarrassed German camp authorities to have to stand aside and take orders from these professional thugs. Camp life took on an ugly and menacing aspect when these boys were engaged in their own particular form of efficiency upgrading.

But do not sell the German soldier short. His ability to rise to the challenge was ultimately proved to be beyond question, as witnessed by an incident which occurred in the summer of 1943 in the camp known as Stalag Luft IV.

For some time lorries had been observed unloading loads of lumber and rolls of barbed wire in a large open space which lay immediately adjacent to our camp. It was unusual to have open fields adjoining the air force prisoner-of-war camps which were generally located in wooded areas, surrounded on all sides by pine trees. Interested prisoners speculated on what

Jerry was up to. The barbed wire appeared to serve no useful purpose, since we were already enclosed by double rows of barbed wire fences spaced three metres apart with the area between filled to a depth of two metres with tangled rolls of the unlovely stuff. Post holes were dug, and large heavy fence posts sprang up overnight. When the workmen commenced stringing the wire along the posts it was obvious that some kind of enclosure was taking shape. An addition to the camp perhaps? If indeed a camp addition, why the strange hourglass shape? It appeared to consist of two oval enclosures with a narrow neck between about the width of the average door. In addition, the opposite ends of each oval had similar door-like passageways, from each of which ran narrow corridors of wire fencing to opposite ends of our camp. From the air the whole contraption must have looked like an enormous brassiere with straps affixed to the north and south extremities of our camp.

The authorities did not keep us in the dark for long. Kommandant Erich Pfeifer made an announcement one morning on parade. "Gentlemen, commencing tomorrow morning appel will be conducted as follows. You will be marched out through the north end of the camp through the recently completed exit to the holding area and will await instructions. That is all. Good day gentlemen." Kommandant Pfeifer always appeared pleased with himself at the enthusiastic response to his twice daily greeting of "good day gentlemen." Each prisoner responded with his own particular ribaldry which usually included such phrases as "drop dead," "Deutschland kaput," "up yours!" and other similar terms of esteem. His satisfied smile was broader than ever that morning as if to say "Now gentlemen of the Allied air forces, let us see if you can falsify our future head counts. German ingenuity will always be equal to your futile cunning and inventiveness."

DO NOT APPROACH THE WARNING WIRE OR IT WILL BE SHOT !

The warning wire clearly defined the boundaries beyond which POWs were not allowed. Sketch first appeared in *The Camp*.

Next morning when the whistle announced *appel* we fell in rather apprehensively, not knowing what to expect. It became obvious very soon that our usual counting by *funfs* was not to take place. Extra guards with Mausers marched in along with our familiar rifle-toting friends. For some reason Pfeifer had decided to speak only German this morning through our *dolmacher* or camp interpreter.

"Gentlemen, you will please proceed single file in an orderly manner through the exit at the north end of the camp." Slowly we moved off, barrack by barrack, until we found ourselves in one of the two oval enclosures. From there we could look back into the now-deserted camp which had taken on a most eerie and forlorn aspect. A strange awareness of being uprooted seemed to fall on us, and I'm sure each prisoner's thoughts matched my own. After all, such as it was, it was our home, and the sooner we were back in familiar surroundings the better. The presence of the extra guards with unslung Mausers did little to relieve the uneasy feelings.

"May I have your attention please? You will now re-form into your accustomed groups and we will get on with the count. It should be quite obvious by now gentlemen that it will be impossible to falsify anything since you will shortly proceed, one at a time, through the narrow exit to the adjoining enclosure and be counted as you pass through." The extra guards had taken up strategic positions at both ends of the passageway. "When I give the word, commence moving through and form up in parade formation in the other enclosure."

We looked at each other as the completely farcical nature of the whole business began to dawn on us. "My God - we are going to be counted like a bunch of bloody sheep!"

"Now gentlemen, now!" The guards took up the cry. "Schnell machen! Schnell machen!" - the German equivalent of "Move it, move it!"

Reluctantly the first few *kriegies* proceeded through. "Schnell, schnell!" was now emphasized with proddings by rifle butts, shoves and an occasional jackboot. The whole scene was utterly ridiculous and mortifying for aircrew personnel from the Royal Air Force. However, the undaunted sense of humour of British soldiers, sailors, and airmen will always rise to any situation. This was no exception. A scurrying airgunner,

Artist's sketch of typical *Appel* held twice daily.

no doubt of Cockney origin, was the first to bleat an outraged "baa, baa" as he side-stepped a shove from an impatient guard on his way through the gauntlet. We looked at each other and expressions of delight spread across each countenance as the opportunity for turning the whole preposterous proceeding into a lark dawned on us. "Baa, baa, baa," we took up the cry. The German guards looked at each other and did their best not to show amusement. The special detail armed with the Mausers did not appear in the least amused as we continued the sometimes excellent, sometimes poorly done imitations of frightened sheep as we dodged our way through the gauntlet of boots and rifle butts. "Baa, baa, baa." The area took on the air of a giant stockyard as sheep are led to their moment of truth by the Judas goat. Kommandant Pfeifer was not amused, and as the moments passed and the din grew ever louder his patience finally wore out.

"Is this the way so-called flyers are supposed to conduct themselves?" he managed to scream above the clamour. "You will cease this nonsense immediately or remain here as long as is necessary to carry out a proper parade. We are in no hurry if you wish to stay here all day." These words from someone in authority succeeded for a few moments in restoring quiet as the procedure commenced again. By now all the guards wore grim expressions of impatience with the way this count was being dragged out. Any prisoner of war foolhardy enough to give vent to an indignant "baa, baa" as he skipped through the enclosure was now helped along with an extra boot on his rear end. As the last prisoner cleared the narrow corridor and joined his comrades and the German guards compared notes on the tally, we wondered what would happen next. The black looks on the guards now made it evident that they were having trouble with the final tally. Angry words were exchanged between them, and Pfeifer stormed out of the enclosure fuming over their apparent inability to reconcile the count.

"You will all stay here and go through this again and again until it is correct," were his instructions to them as he disappeared, forgetting his customary "Good morning, gentlemen."

With Kommandant Pfeifer gone all further communications between guards and prisoners required the assistance of an interpreter. The apoplectic remarks of the frustrated German NCO in charge, even when softened by translation, left no doubt that we had better co-operate or face a long and unpleasant afternoon. The count was to be done over again and we had better move quickly and obediently or suffer appropriate reprisals. Slowly the afternoon wore on as bored guards once again took up the monotonous count. So far no one had been foolhardy enough to venture an outraged "baa, baa" as he scurried back through the narrow opening to the original holding area. However there is safety in numbers, and as the count approached the mid-point, which found approximately equal numbers of *kriegies* in each compound, the cries of assorted barnyard livestock began again. This time they included mating calls of lovelorn cows, sheep, heifers, shorthorns, rams, sows, amorous bulls, and various other domestic animals as we bleated, bellowed, oinked and mooed messages back and forth between enclosures. The fury of the guards was tempered by an obstinate determination to complete an accurate tally. With gritted teeth they stubbornly carried on as the late-afternoon shadows lengthened and the uncontrollable din turned the once-pastoral countryside into a scene of saturnalia, accompanied by a sound-track from a stockyard, playing at full volume to a most unappreciative and captive audience.

Finally, the count approached an end as the last prisoner stumbled from the effects of a propelling boot into the enclosure. Guards, now with rifles and machine-guns in ready position, moved quickly to concentrate their attentions on the assembled flyers and began to prod us roughly into some sort of orderly arrangement. The fun was evidently over, and discretion asserted itself as the now quiet ranks waited the outcome of the tally. Surely they would not try another count! A third performance would almost inevitably lead to a nasty confrontation, and in their present mood could easily result in bloodshed. Even German discipline had its flash-point and it had been tested today most thoroughly. The thoughts uppermost in everyone's mind, prisoner and guard alike, must have been similar as we allowed ourselves to be herded back to camp to end this bizarre day. What of the future? Was this ludicrous performance to be repeated the following day? Was the head count to turn into an absurd burlesque performance, acted out daily for the amusement of recalcitrant prisoners and accompanied by the mounting feelings of rage experienced by our sometimes trigger-happy guards?

Pfeifer's thoughts must have been running along similar lines. Next morning he announced, "We will have no repetition of yesterday's disgraceful proceedings. The German army has more important duties to attend to than to attempt to instill military pride into the minds of men who are obviously completely lacking in discipline, and who are unwilling or incapable of acting in a soldierly manner. You will return to your quarters and think about what I have said. Regular parade procedure will be re-established, and remember gentlemen, if you do not co-operate we have ways of making you do so. That is all!"

Thus ended this frolicsome incident. A small victory for us, admittedly. But add to this the numerous other equally small victories and it leaves no doubt: by the time hostilities came to an end, the German army was thoroughly sick of the sight of

Great Escape foes recall old days

The man who engineered the "Great Escape" of 76 war prisoners from a German camp 26 years ago and the man whose job it was to keep them inside the barbed wire drank together last night in the officers' mess of the Canadian Forces Staff School on Avenue Rd.

Hermann Glemnitz, 71, in Toronto for the 25th anniversary this weekend of the Ex-Air Force Prisoners of War Association at the Royal York Hotel, claimed he knew the prisoners were digging the tunnel.

"Then how come you couldn't find it?" said Wally Floody, 52, the one-time hard-rock miner who mastermind-ed the digging of the 320-foot tunnel.

Glemnitz a former Luftwaffe staff-sergeant, was in charge of security at StalagLuft III, the camp where the escape was made.

"Well," he laughed, "maybe I wasn't trying too hard. Or maybe I felt sorry for you. Or maybe you were just too clever for me."

"You were tough," said Floody.

Glemnitz, who worked as a Royal Air Force interpreter after the war, replied: "I had a tough job to do."

All but three of the men who escaped from Stalag Luft III, in March, 1944, were recaptured. Fifty of them, including some Canadians, were shot by the Gestapo on orders from Hitler.

—Star Photo

THE GUARD AND THE PRISONER
Herman Glemnitz (left) and Wally Floody

Extract from *Toronto Star*, 1970. Staff-sergeant Hermann Glemnitz visits with former enemies.

air force blue and was only too glad to turn to the much less challenging task of rebuilding Germany.

Twenty-six years later at the Royal York Hotel in Toronto, a reunion of ex-air force prisoners of war took place. Among the invited guests was former *Luftwaffe* staff-sergeant Hermann Glemnitz, then seventy-one years of age. He had been in charge of security at various prison camps in Germany, and was well aware of the many problems which continually arose in the performance of his distasteful duty. He was the man entrusted with security who had no real stomach for the job: a decent type discharging an unpleasant responsibility. He was respected by his superiors and by prisoners alike. As he drank together with former tunneling mastermind Wally Floody, he recalled his mixed feelings of respect and sympathy for us, tempered by a soldier's desire to do his duty honourably.

CHAPTER TEN
The Poker Match (or The Gentle Art of Blackmail)

One of the highlights of prisoner-of-war existence, probably second only to parcel issue and mail from home, was the daily reading of the BBC news. To those of us who today take hourly newscasts for granted, and only half listen while our daily measure of disasters, hijackings, political assassinations, starvation or terrorism is served to us, the importance of daily news reports is much less. After all, who needs the depressing statistics which are forced upon us with such regularity by the media?

Incredible as it may seem it was not always so! Prisoners of war were literally starved for news. We lived for the day when our ordeal would be over, and naturally seized upon any scrap of good news concerning the war as an indication that our eventual freedom was nearer. German newspapers and camp public-address systems fed us daily on the glorious triumphs of the Third Reich. If they were to be believed it was only a matter of time until the swastika flew proudly in any corner of the world which was not already under the heel of the land of the rising sun.

Propaganda is an immensely powerful weapon, and nowhere was it used to better advantage than in the German press. The Goebbels' machine, with fiendish cleverness, transformed enormous war losses and battle defeats into trivial pinpricks and "strategic withdrawals" that the gullible German public accepted eagerly. They did so because Goebbels understood the first and most basic principal of propaganda: tell the people what they want to hear.

However it is a two-edged sword, since promises unfulfilled can be more damaging than unpleasant truths. It is also true that the British and Americans used this weapon with success, but not with such flagrant deceit as did Germany. It is for this reason that we as prisoners of war, having access to both news sources, were perhaps in the best position to make predictions about the war's end. We became armchair strategists and made comprehensive analyses of all the areas of conflict, regularly inflicting our opinions of the abilities of our war leaders on anyone who would listen.

The BBC news was most definitely not taken for granted. It was received only at the utmost risk. Radio receivers were forbidden and dangerous to use. The penalties were severe, and could include even execution if it could be proved that we were engaged in intelligence activities. The problems of assembling radios were enormous. Wireless parts were virtually non-existent and replacement of burned-out tubes was equally challenging. As clever as our technical expertise became, to the point where short-wave receivers could be built and assembled from bits of tin and wire, it was impossible to build a radio tube or "valve" as it was called. We were forced to rely on other methods to acquire these essential components. I will return to this later.

Very few highly trusted men were assigned to the job of picking up the noon-hour British Broadcasting Corporation news report. Their identity was classified information. They did their work in an atmosphere of cloak-and-dagger secrecy, and very seldom operated from the same locale twice running.

116

When the radio signals were turned off, the various components of the illegal radio receiver were returned to their several hiding places until required again. The news was never taken down in plain language, but in code which was frequently changed. Anyone who might accidentally see the hand-written bulletin would be unable to make sense of it, and would most likely mistake it for the scribblings of someone studying for an examination in mathematics.

Further elaborate precautions were taken when the daily news was read to us. A prison camp was made up of anywhere from half a dozen to as many as fifty or more separate huts or barracks. In a typical air force camp the number of barracks was usually around ten. The news was read to each hut separately, and security was, of course, very tight. Sentinels were placed at each end of the building, and two more were placed at the windows on each side before the news was read to an attentive audience. Even the area beneath the floor had to be "swept" to insure there were no German ferrets (men trained to search for tunnels). These ferrets pretended no knowledge of English, but were skilled in both languages and had very inquisitive noses and big ears.

As clever as the radio boffins were, they could not replace a burned-out tube, and so were forced to resort to other means of acquiring them. This is a true story of one particular incident, and is representative of similar refinements of the art of blackmail as practised and perfected on our hapless assortment of guards.

The German soldier was issued a daily cigarette ration of seven cigarettes which was to last him for twenty-four hours. Those of us who have attempted to cut down on smoking by limiting our lot to a specified few must know how difficult this can become. The temptation to reach automatically for a cigarette, and the soothing therapy afforded in the ritual of lighting up, is not easy to forego. This method of cutting back is seldom successful and most of us fall by the wayside as we find the ordeal too much to endure. Consider then the plight of the German guard forced to endure interminably this form of privation. In addition, he was unpleasantly aware that we prisoners of war, under his heel so to speak, were enjoying a seemingly unlimited supply of cigarettes. This was very often true. Cigarettes could be sent from Canada and from England very cheaply, and usually in cartons of three hundred or one thousand. It was the most usual form of remembering a son or husband by loved ones back home. When parcels were getting through it was not unusual for individuals to have several thousand fags on hand. It was also true that in hard times we went for weeks or months on end without a comforting puff and were reduced to smoking dried tea-leaves after they had been used many times over for tea.

One of the problems encountered in keeping our secret radios operative was the necessity of cultivating a new lot of guards when we were moved to a different camp. The art of blackmail had to be as varied as the types of guards encountered, and had to begin from square one in each new camp. It also had to be tailored to the situations and the varying degrees of loyalty to the fatherland manifested by our captors. It was indeed quite a delicate problem, since obvious attempts to tempt a patriotic German soldier very often resulted in outraged refusal of a proffered bribe, and a consequent visit to the camp prison by the unfortunate *kriegie* who stood accused of attempting to corrupt the German honour.

Word had come down that our daily newscasts were likely to cease unless some vital tubes could be replaced in our rapidly fading receiver. It was essential that some of the guards be tested as to their abilities to withstand temptation in the form of a packet or so of English cigarettes in return for items we would require from time to time. How to soften them up? These were new and strange guards and the way had to be prepared with some subtlety. Blowing smoke in the face of some poor German soldier at three o'clock in the afternoon when he had smoked the last of his allotted seven at two o'clock was ruled out as being rather obvious.

So a poker game was to be arranged. It was to be like no other card-game usually played, where the allowable wager might typically consist of a two-cigarette limit. This was to be a carefully orchestrated game, played for the benefit of our bored guards who relieved the monotony of their uninspiring existence by watching with interest the unending games of bridge and poker. There were to be six players, all of whom would be smokers. It was to be played when two guards named Walther Braun and Ernst Langer were on duty. They both enjoyed a quiet smoke, and were both considered to be susceptible to temptation. They had both made it obvious that they were fed up with the war and longed to get home. They were too old for active service and had no particular loyalty to the cause. They functioned as members of the army mainly because of harsh German discipline. Their only wish was to return home to Frau Braun and Frau Langer.

The game was to be in full swing by late afternoon when Walther and Ernst would have almost certainly smoked the last of their meagre ration, and their resistance would be at its lowest ebb. For this game the normal two-cigarette limit was to be removed. This was definitely not a friendly game played for peanuts. The stakes were to be high.

The game started slowly with the six regulars playing a few tentative hands for the usual nominal bets. As soon as Walther and Ernst made their appearance in the hut all six players lit up cigarettes. Like moths to flame the German guards were drawn to the area where the game was in progress, joining the half-dozen or so other spectators.

"Why don't we make it interesting?" suggested Alex. "Let's raise the limit and play five-card stud only."

"Suits me," responded George and he looked at the other four players questioningly. The other card-players indicated their agreement. "Sure, why not? What would you suggest?" asked Jimmy.

Jimmy was dark and good-looking. He had a deep scar, received when his chin had made contact with the instrument panel of his mosquito fighter-bomber on a crash-landing. He was attempting to hide the scar by growing a Van Dyke beard, and it added to his swashbuckling appearance. He looked every inch a gambler. Ernst and Walther looked on with a mixture of interest and resentment at the flippant manner in which precious cigarettes were being treated by the prisoners. Dying for a smoke as they were, even just a puff or two, the sight of six enemy flyers turning the air blue with tobacco smoke was almost more than they could endure.

And so it was decided to remove any limit on the wagers. The men interrupted the game long enough to replenish their supplies of cigarettes. They each returned to the table with several unopened cartons of cigarettes which they placed beside them to the astonishment of the two Germans who looked on in amazement at the vast amount of wealth displayed. Jimmy casually lit a cigarette as they opened the bidding on the first round of the game of stud poker. He glanced at his down card, slid it back under his visible ace of diamonds, ground his almost fresh cigarette into the ashtray and slid five fresh cigarettes into the centre of the table. "I'll open for five," he declared. Each of the other five card-players solemnly matched Jimmy's opening bet. Another card was dealt face up to each man. George's hand now showed two sevens, the others had nothing much while Jimmy received a king to go with his visible ace. George quickly slid an unopened package of twenty into the pot. "That's what my pair of sevens are worth," he grinned.

"Okay George," replied Jimmy. "I'll stay with you," he said as he slid another unopened twenty across the table. Three players folded their cards and withdrew. Alex looked at his six and ten of hearts and slowly slid a package of twenty into the pot. There were now over eighty cigarettes on the table. The two Germans looked at each other and swallowed. Ernst slowly shook his head as the three other players lit up and exhaled a bluish haze of luxurious Virginia tobacco smoke.

On the next round Jimmy received a jack of clubs and Alex a small useless card, while George's two sevens were unimproved. As Alex withdrew, George bet a further twenty which was matched by Jimmy, whose hand showed the possibility of a four-card straight. Under the rules of the five-card stud game they were playing, a straight would beat George's two sevens. There was now one card turned down in front of each player while three cards lay face up. One more card remained to be dealt to each player. More than one hundred cigarettes were on the table and the situation was tense. Ernst and Walther appeared to be almost beside themselves. The desire for a smoke was overpowering for the unfortunate men as George and Jimmy each took a fresh cigarette and lit up before dealing the final card. It was obvious the two guards were completely softened and ripe for the kill. Slowly George slid a card across to Jimmy. It was a queen of diamonds and his face-card straight of ace, king, queen and jack would beat George's pair. George flipped a card from the top of the deck. It was a seven! He now had three sevens showing. Without a moment's hesitation he tossed a full carton of two hundred into the pot. But Jimmy didn't fold. He calmly slid an unopened carton onto the table.

"I'll match you George," he replied. "And I'll raise you another two hundred." He reached under the table and tossed another carton of Players into the pot. The spectators edged closer. Ernst and Walther stood in a state of near shock. The poker pot contained three month's issue of cigarettes to a German private.

George carefully studied Jimmy's cards. If Jimmy's hidden card was a ten, it would beat his three sevens. On the other hand, a straight was no good against four sevens. "I'm calling you, Jimmy," he said as he pushed a carton of two hundred across the table.

"Unless you have a seven hidden, I've got you, George." Jimmy flipped over his hidden card revealing a ten which filled in his five-card straight.

"It's yours, Jimmy," said George as he pushed the entire pot containing four cartons, several packages of twenty and a few loose fags to his opponent. Jimmy was magnanimous in victory.

"Here, Fritz, have a smoke, you poor sod," and he offered Walther a loose cigarette which the guard accepted gratefully. As he lit the cigarette for the German soldier George motioned to Ernst, the other guard. "Kommen sie mit mier," he whispered to him. The guard followed George expectantly, giving a realistic imitation of a trained poodle awaiting a choice tidbit from its master.

George led the German to a small empty room at the end of the barrack, which had by prior arrangement been vacated by the hut leader. What Ernst did not know, of course, was that the entire game had been arranged for his benefit. The large number of cigarettes which he had seen wagered on the climactic finish to the poker game would be returned to the original owners. All Ernst could understand was that the prisoners had *viel cigaretten* and he badly wanted a share of them. George's offer of a smoke was eagerly accepted by the guard. For a moment or two the men smoked in silence, seated at opposite ends of the small table. Finally George broke in upon the German soldier's quiet moment of enjoyment. "You know, Ernst, there are more cigarettes where that came from." Ernst did not need to be reminded of this obvious fact in the light of what he and Walther Braun had just seen in the barrack. The German said nothing but regarded George questioningly, waiting for him to continue. He was no fool and knew there had to be a catch somewhere, but his loyalty to a fading cause had long since weakened as had that of many of the older soldiers. They were not front-line troops, and were really only going through the motions of soldiering, but still remained in the firm grasp of German army discipline.

George pulled two radio tubes from his pocket and placed them on the table between them. The guard looked nervously around and made a motion as if to leave. It was now obvious to him what the price was to be; but supplying radio equipment to the prisoners was an offence which could end his army career in front of a firing squad.

George spoke very slowly and evenly. "A carton of two hundred fags, one hundred for each tube if you can duplicate these two tired ones Ernst." George slid a slip of paper across the table with size and code numbers, and pocketed the tubes. The guard picked up the paper and slowly folded it, placing it in his hat lining. "I will think about it. It will not be easy, and of course very dangerous." The Englishman lit another cigarette and offered one to Ernst who accepted a light. Again the two men - the tired, disenchanted remnant of German armed forces, and the young English flyer - smoked in curious companionable silence, strangely united because each had something the other needed. George felt a sense of power not unmixed with sympathy for the older man who had been placed in such an unfortunate situation merely to be able to enjoy the comfort of a simple cigarette.

At length Ernst stood up, having butted his smoke carefully and placed the unsmoked portion in his pocket. "Ja, I must think. I will let you know." He turned and left the room to rejoin Walther who had been idly chatting in the hut with the prisoners, enjoying a cup of instant coffee with real sugar. Walther was less bright than Ernst and was not at all suspicious of his partner's disappearance. The two German guards moved off to resume their interrupted duties. As they left the hut the assembled prisoners looked at George, who merely raised his hands with the fingers crossed and smiled, shrugging his shoulders ever so slightly.

Ernst Langer was not long in making up his mind. He was not a fool and was aware of the possible consequences of his actions; but on the other hand he only needed to be careful not to flaunt his sudden wealth. To be seen in local beer halls or army barracks smoking English cigarettes was not in itself incriminating. Most of the guards accepted hand-outs from time to time for small favours. Ernst need only be reasonably prudent. He must be careful to make his purchases in Berlin or Breslau, or some large town where he was not recognized. Other than that the risk was relatively small.

A few days later the transaction was made and Ernst went off duty with close to a month's supply of English cigarettes distributed in various packets and recesses of his greatcoat, while once again the BBC news was clandestinely received and read to the British airmen.

But whether he was immediately aware of it or not, Ernst Langer was firmly hooked. As long as the British flyers remained in that camp the replenishment of contraband wireless parts was assured. Should he refuse to co-operate, the screws which he had allowed to be placed on him would be tightened by the prisoners. The next time the required items might include anything from German army cap badges to compasses, detailed maps or ration books, or even blank identity cards. The threat of revealing his complicity to the *kommandant*, whether real or feigned, would remain. Ernst Langer and others like him in other camps would remain at the mercy of men whom they believed were ruthless enough to resort to blackmail to get what they needed. Whether this was in fact true is something else. There were many prison camps in Germany holding men desperate enough for anything.

Fortunately it never happened to Ernst. He was still around when we moved off to a new camp. I am sure he raised a silent glass to our departure and swore never to allow the *Englische fliegers* to tempt him again!

CHAPTER ELEVEN
From East Prussia Without Love

In the summer of 1944 the tide of the war had at long last turned in favour of the combined might of Russia and the Allies. On every front German forces found themselves being driven relentlessly back. The small foothold which had been gained on D Day had solidified and spread like a fast-growing cancer and was poised for a final crushing blow to German arms. On the Eastern Front Soviet divisions had pushed the once invincible might of Germany from its war-ravaged lands, and were now fighting on German soil, a situation which was new to Germany. She had never in recent history, even during the war years 1914-1918, had to defend her own towns and villages from the devastating effects of artillery and hand-to-hand combat. While it was true that the large industrial and military targets had been practically demolished by air raids and her major cities lay in smoking ruins, she had never before had to surrender the smaller towns, villages and hamlets to advancing enemy forces.

The German army retreated like a snarling, spitting, badly wounded animal, determined to sell itself dearly. High-level policy had dictated that there was to be no surrender. Although most of the high-ranking commanders of Hitler's forces had now realized the futility of the sacrifices they and their men were making, they had little choice but to obey orders and fight on.

As a result, the mood of German forces responsible for guarding Allied prisoners of war had undergone a drastic change. Their previous relatively humane treatment had now been replaced by grudging, and in some cases merely token adherence to the terms of the Geneva Conventions which governed the conduct and treatment of Allied flyers who had fallen into their hands. Those who escaped could no longer expect to be returned unharmed to prison camp upon recapture, to undergo the standard twenty-one days in the cooler. Proclamations signed by the camp *kommandant* appeared on the notice-board stating that any attempts to escape would now incur the death penalty by order of supreme command. Reprisals for misdemeanours were cruel and harsh. It was very definitely an ugly and dangerous time to be at the mercy of German forces, alleviated only by the fact that as hostages the prisoners were valuable property, and therefore a high card which Germany could still hold in reserve for a final desperate play in the deadly game of world conflict. The stakes were very high indeed - survival as a nation.

The Russian three-pronged attack upon the heart of Germany was proceeding as planned. The northern pincer had turned slightly towards the Baltic coast with the eventual intention of turning south and joining the central prong of the attack, to unite forces and drive their combined might straight towards Berlin. In doing so, vast numbers of men and amounts of material would be encircled. A secondary effect would be to cut off the north-east portion of Germany known as East Prussia, where Hitler's strategic headquarters was located near Königsberg, as was Stalag Luft VI, an Allied air force prison camp which contained approximately five hundred British, Canadian and other Allied airmen. As prison camps go it was average. Up to now we had been more or less left alone, subject only to routine roll-calls and standard disciplinary measures. Things were about to change for the worse, suddenly and savagely.

It was too late for German authorities to evacuate the camp by rail. The Russian advance had completely cut off all lines. The only chance of holding the prisoners, or more correctly hostages, as we now really were, was to march the men north to Memel, a seaport on the Baltic coast, and from there ship them out by water to Stettin in north-central Germany. We were not allowed to take anything that could not be carried on our bodies. It was to be a tough march, and we were advised to travel light. A blanket, the few possessions which would fit in a knapsack or bedroll, and the available rations would be all we could expect to carry. The march itself was relatively uneventful, although the hatred of the civilian population was very evident as we passed through the small villages and hamlets. The guards had instructions to deliver us safely to Memel and found themselves at times having to defend us from savage reprisals by their own people who had suffered desperately from Allied air attacks, and who were eager to get their hands on, and even lynch, any prisoner who could not keep up.

After three days we arrived in Memel, and were herded to the dock area and brought to a halt alongside an ancient rusting hulk of a ship which had been temporarily relieved of its task of carrying coal through the Baltic. The Baltic Sea was a lifeline much used by Germany for movement of war supplies, and had been heavily mined by aircraft of Bomber Command. The prospects of a journey of several days' duration in the hold of this coal barge was most dreadful. It became nothing short of terrifying when we commenced boarding the ship and became aware of the conditions under which we were to travel. One by one we descended a single steel ladder into the hold. This ladder represented our sole means of escape in the event of striking a mine or receiving a hit from either a torpedo or a direct hit from air attack. It is unlikely that a single prisoner would have been able to reach the deck in time to attempt to save himself.

The interior of the hold was cavernous, dark, thick with black coal-dust and lacking in the most elementary facilities for sanitation. There was no water, no toilet other than a bucket lowered on a rope which was pulled up and dumped over the side when full. The guards huddled on deck and ignored our requests for some form of relief from these intolerable conditions. The weather was very warm, the interior of the steel hull was hot, and the air in it heavy with sweat, urine and human excrement. Bread was sent down once or twice, but few of us felt any inclination to eat in the stinking semi-darkness. Smoking was permitted since there was minimum fire hazard. Consequently the gloom was thickened by a blue haze which somehow helped to mask the miasmic overpowering stench.

The ship had been fitted with electric degaussing equipment designed to fend off magnetic mines. The apparatus was passed over the outside of the metal hull at regular intervals. It was held in place and guided along the underwater exterior portion of the ship by large steel chains which caused such a clattering din in the echoing hold of the ship that the nerves of the men, already frayed, became stretched to the breaking point. To this day I have a vivid memory of attempting to get a light for my cigarette from a comrade whose hand was shaking so badly that the unlit cigarette and the lighted match could make contact only with great difficulty. There was some grim humour in the situation and we both laughed nervously at the absurdity of our inability to perform this common friendly gesture. Even today, forty years later when we meet at reunions, I never fail to ask Brian for a light and we solemnly re-enact the little charade.

After three days and two nights the ship arrived at the Baltic port of Stettin, where a line of boxcars had been drawn up on the pier. We were transferred rapidly in the now familiar conditions of fifty men to each car, with two armed guards inside and two more on the roof. We remained there for another night. Shortly after dark the port of Stettin suffered an air attack and our guards departed to the shelters, locking the doors and leaving us alone. The noise of the raid and the close proximity of the anti-aircraft guns, which fired unceasingly, combined to add to the ordeal. We merely sat, waited, and prayed. Luck was with us as none of the boxcars was hit.

The following day found us still standing on the pier. Undoubtedly the raid of the previous night had caused disruption in rail service to the dock area. Railway lines, always a prime target for raids, had been torn up by the raid, and not until slave workers had restored the tracks could we move out of the area. The following morning, just after dawn, a series of jolting crashes was felt as we were hooked to a locomotive. Shortly afterwards we began to move slowly, and with frequent long stops, away from the port of Stettin.

We were now heading south-east in the general direction of Berlin. It was apparent that the journey was to be a relatively short one, since, as hostages, we would not be relocated too far east, which would necessitate a further move westwards away from advancing Russian armies. This was a positive factor and gave us a lift in morale. Although we were not enduring the kind of hardship we had suffered on the sea voyage, train travel under these conditions was very uncomfortable. The knowledge that all moving freight trains were targets for over-eager fighter pilots did not make the trip any easier.

We were, of course, never told where we were headed, but by keeping our eyes on the sun and by obtaining an occasional glimpse of a station name as we moved south-eastwards, we were able to get a rough idea of where we were heading.

By early afternoon the train came to a dead stop. The doors were slid open by the guards and we were harshly ordered to get out and line up with all our gear. The sun was a welcome sight to eyes which had become accustomed to the gloomy interiors of the boxcars, but it was a boiling hot day. The German major in charge appeared to be on the verge of apoplexy as he screamed at us, and waved his pistol wildly in a display of German fury, contempt, and hatred towards us which was evidently intended to cow us, or to frighten us into complete submission to his hysterical commands. Of more concern, however, was the changed nature of the guards detailed to patrol the column. Our former guards, rather run-down dead-beat types not fit for active service, had completely disappeared. They had been replaced by young marines with fixed bayonets on their rifles. The number of guards had also been tripled: I estimated roughly two hundred of them. Every other one held a leash on the end of which an Alsation or Dobermann guard dog tugged, snarled and barked excitedly. It was an ominous situation. Where were we? Where were we headed? Was there even a prison camp nearby? What was in store for us?

With much shouting and prodding by rifle butts we were ordered to form up into fives to be counted. A large metal supply box was unloaded from the back of a parked army vehicle and the guards were ordered in German: "Nehmen sie die Handschelle." It quickly dawned on those of us with some knowledge of German what was about to happen. We were to be handcuffed! With speed and efficiency it was accomplished by the maliciously grinning marines who were quite clearly enjoying these special duties to which they had been detailed. We were not simply handcuffed left hand to right hand. As the guards moved down the assembled column, in each rank of five men, the outside pairs were handcuffed in such a way as to leave the centre prisoner free of chains in each row of fives. I was fortunate. I was in the centre of a row and escaped the shackling, and breathed a silent prayer of thanks. It still remained to be determined whether by escaping the handcuffs I had gained any particular advantage, but it gave me a degree of comfort in the knowledge that to some extent I was still master of my own fate, whatever that was to be.

The senior NCO Sergeant Clarke insisted on an explanation from the German major. With cool persistence he pressed for a reason for these proceedings and demanded to be informed where we were going, and reminded him of the rights to which we were entitled. The answer was a display of raging, ranting abuse and a further string of German obscenities with a frequent referral in part English to "murdering Englische Schwein" accompanied by threatening, waving, and pointing of his German Luger pistol in the general direction of the shaken prisoners.

The spluttering major now barked some command to his men who ordered us to get moving and the long column moved off in the oppressive heat of the afternoon sun. The road led off to a heavily wooded area and very soon the railway siding and the drawn-up train had disappeared from view. Suddenly a volley of shots rang out from the rear of the column. It was a pre-arranged signal for the guards. They lunged at us with fixed bayonets yelling at us "Now you English pigs - run!" accompanied by a string of German oaths. It was almost impossible to escape the jabs, and many men received deep flesh-wounds to thighs, buttocks, and arms. In addition, the snarling and barking dogs had been released to snap at us and to tear at our heels as we ran. These dogs were vicious and trained to kill. We had actually witnessed, in previous camps, the training of these animals and were now experiencing firsthand the results of the savagery which had been bred into them.

The handcuffed prisoners suffered more from this treatment since attempts to dodge jabbing bayonets or snarling dogs were made more difficult for the men who were chained together and consequently impeded in their movement. Once again I gave fervent thanks for being unchained. One of the brutes singled me out for attack. I stopped and waited for it, and as the animal lunged at me I aimed a perfectly timed kick and caught him fully on the side of his head. My adrenalin was flowing and the strength of the kick turned him aside. The dog ran off in obvious pain and surprise.

We were now headed down a long straight stretch of road hemmed in on both sides by dark forests. Suddenly we became aware that there were men in the woods. Every few hundred feet was a crouching figure positioned behind a machine-gun. The guns swivelled and followed us menacingly as we passed. Now a terrifying thought gripped each one of us as we ran grimly on. It began to appear as though no prison camp existed, and that this was to be the end for us all. As each man in turn realized the desperateness of the situation, he started ditching his gear. The scene that followed was indescribable and will be forever etched in my brain. Never will I forget the panic-stricken look of a fellow prisoner urging us to scatter for our lives or be mowed down. The road was strewn with blankets, kitbags, books and Red Cross parcels which had been abandoned. To add to the chaos some of the men were exhausted and were collapsing, unable to run further. The prisoners who were handcuffed tried to help each other as best they could. It was an obstacle course like none other as we ran on, attempting to dodge the equipment or comrades lying in the road. I glanced at the panting German marine alongside of me who was obviously tiring and had stopped wielding his bayonet and was now more concerned with merely keeping station. I had a strange sense of elation as I realized I could outlast him if need be as I matched him stride for stride. I had made a habit of doing my best to stay fit, eating wisely and refusing any extra grub which was of doubtful origin. I felt a surge of strength derived from the knowledge that a hand-picked member of the so-called master race was showing such obvious signs of being much less. Our eyes met briefly and he sensed my feeling of contempt, I'm quite sure, because he averted his eyes from mine.

By this time I had jettisoned my kitbag with my few bits of belongings and remaining food rations, but was determined not to part with my bedroll which was draped around my shoulders. My canteen of fresh water bumped against my side as I ran but that also I decided to hang onto.

"Whatever you do, don't panic," was the word that was passed from man to man. "Jerry is trying to get us to make a break for it." This would give him an excuse for opening fire from the machine-guns which lined the road on both sides. They would claim we had been shot attempting to escape and thus remain protected by international law. This knowledge helped to calm some of the men who were close to playing into their hands by making a mad dash for it. It was much to the credit of these cooler heads that not a single one of us made the attempt.

On and on we ran: gasping, sweat-soaked prisoners and equally exhausted guards. Many of us had lost quite a lot of blood from bayonet wounds. Others had received bites from the wildly excited guard dogs. Still others lay on the road - their fate unknown to us. Under the blazing heat of that mid-afternoon sun on a lonely road somewhere in north-eastern Germany the exhausted, hopeless men stumbled on until suddenly a clearing appeared. The trees fell away on both sides of the road to reveal a large open area. In the centre of this wide plain was a sight that we never imagined could be such a marvellous one to behold! There were rows of barrack-like huts and an open area surrounded by double rows of barbed wire with guard towers spaced at intervals around the perimeter. We gazed with heartfelt feelings of relief at this wondrously familiar sight. A prison camp did exist! We had at last arrived at the end of this nightmarish journey which had lasted for the better part of a week: first the march, then the boat ride, followed by the train and culminating in the final insane run up the road. Our ordeal, however, was not quite over.

As we moved inside the open gates between the rows of marines, we were ordered to form up into fives for counting. We obeyed the order, and I seized the opportunity to sneak a drink of water from my canteen. I lifted it and began to drink, and felt a blow to the back of my neck from the side of a rifle butt which caused me to stagger, nearly knocking me senseless. Gradually the fog cleared and I found myself looking at the marine who had read my thoughts back on the road. He had no doubt salvaged his honour by slamming his rifle butt into the neck of this unarmed prisoner-of-war. Although stunned, I was not seriously hurt.

In later years at prisoner-of-war reunions the "Run up the road" is remembered by those who took part in it with a sort of unexplainable zest, and with a certain amount of pride in the knowledge that we had endured. We had not played into the hands of our captors by panicking and scattering for our lives. We had remained cool and disciplined and had cheated them of their chance to slaughter us by claiming under the Geneva Conventions that we had been shot while attempting to escape. It was a small victory, but a victory nevertheless. The elaborate precautions, the specially trained marines, the armed assassins in the woods, the dogs, the handcuffs had been beaten by the spirit of the Allied flyers. We had indeed won out on that July afternoon so long ago. I shall always remember with a great deal of pride how we handled ourselves on that lonely road which for a while appeared to lead to nowhere but humiliation and oblivion.

CHAPTER TWELVE
Rhineland Wine, Vintage 1944

To begin with, let me make it very clear that this tale is not
intended for those who profess to be wine connoisseurs. It is
not for those who are fortunate enough to have acquired the
discriminating taste which enables one to appreciate the fine
shades of flavour, aging, bouquet, body and colour which
render the peculiar richness of a Burgundy preferable to a
more austere Bordeaux. No doubt the earthy, rough-spoken,
muscular construction worker drinking *vin ordinaire* at a Paris
bistro at mid-morning break would have more reason to relish
this anecdote. If your tastes lie somewhere in between,
however, I hope you will find it entertaining and amusing.

A basic knowledge of high school chemistry is all that is
required to manufacture a drink with an alcoholic content.
The simplest method is to boil something that contains sugar
and distil the alcohol which reaches boiling-point before the
water. To do this, it is necessary to build some sort of still. This
is not beyond the technical capabilities of resourceful men who
are eager to try their hand at home-brew, and are not unduly
worried about the possible effect on their insides, or the purity
of the alcohol which has a nasty habit of mutating into other
more sinister derivatives if not properly controlled during the
process of distillation.

Another method is to begin with a starchy product and encourage formation of sugar from which alcohol can be obtained. Since prisoner-of-war diet consisted almost entirely of potatoes, a certain number could be spared to fuel our sometimes dangerous experiments, as will be seen.

The making of wine takes a substantial amount of time, and even under ideal conditions many wine makers today proudly serve cloudy and dubious concoctions to unfortunate guests who dutifully and bravely swallow, murmuring suitable polite affirmation as to its full-bodied flavour while searching desperately for a means to dump it, without offending their triumphantly beaming host. Under prison camp conditions, with raisins substituting for grapes or grape juice, the results were usually disastrous. However, the resulting brew did actually produce the desired effect of intoxication.

During my three and a half years as a prisoner of war I was involved in all three types of alcohol production but wisely refrained from drinking the product from two of the experiments. Today I appreciate a glass of wine but, far from being a connoisseur, I am informed that I have no taste for good wine, only a taste for any wine. Perhaps that is because, having experienced how badly a wine can be made, I now relish by comparison the wines which are found on the shelves of wine stores in Canada. My motto is simply to appreciate each and every wine for its own sake.

One day George, my combine partner, decided that he and I were going to try our hand at making potato whisky. He had been in the bag since Dunkirk and we had become friends while we were engaged in an identity swap. He had exchanged identities with an air force sergeant, while I had done likewise with a British private - but that is another story. In the early days of the war George had been able to more than hold his own when any occasion arose for serious drinking. He was a tough customer, but a loyal friend. If he wanted to sacrifice some of our spud ration to experiment with whisky-making I was willing to try.

"It's simple," he said. "All we do is make a mash of raw potato, since we don't have any grain, add water, boil it and then let it ferment during which the starch in the potato turns to sugar, then to alcohol, finally we distil it and presto we have a smooth whisky!" It sounded simple and we began our preparation. The problem would be finding a suitable container in which to store the finished product for the aging process. We finally settled for a metal wash-basin, since procuring a wooden barrel was out of the question. The first problem was to exchange our daily ration of potatoes, which were issued to us already cooked in their jackets, for raw potatoes. This was not that easy, since potatoes issued to the cookhouse were tightly controlled and accountable for by mess personnel. George and I, however, were able to trade in our cooked ration on three consecutive days for an equal supply of uncooked ones. The staff in the kitchen were a bit curious but we were not about to enlighten them. We merely explained that George had not had fish and chips for three years, and wanted to blow three day's ration on a feast of proper chips fried in margarine served with a tin of Red Cross issue pilchards in tomato sauce. We carefully scraped them, as peeling would have wasted valuable starch. Using a sharp knife, we cut them into minute sections to which boiling water was added. We then set the resulting mash under our bunk and allowed it to stand.

Three days later there was no doubt that something was working. The concoction was giving off a distinct odour of fermentation which gave rise to plaintive queries and complaints from the occupants of neighbouring bunks. We ignored the comments and references to malodorous decomposing flesh, and commenced preparation for the next step which was to bring the mash to a boil and condense the vapour given off by leading it through a suitable pipe made of hammered-out Klim tins over which I poured a stream of cold water. In theory the liquid which condensed from this stream would be pure grain alcohol.

George was confident by now that success was imminent and gave a show of lip-smacking appreciation as he eagerly sampled the first few precious drops which condensed from the brew. By evening we had collected almost a pint which was poured carefully into the wash-basin and placed under our bunks to be sampled the next day, which was George's birthday. We were well satisfied with our efforts and went to sleep that night looking forward with pleasure to an evening meal the next day which would be preceded by our own private happy hour and washed down with good whisky.

George was up early the next morning and as he rolled from his bunk his eye fell on the wash-basin which was exactly where it had been placed the previous evening. It was empty! "What the blazes?" His broad Lancashire dialect rose to a threatening roar. "Who the hell pinched my whisky?" I took a closer look under the bunk. The whole area around our bed was damp and smelled vaguely of disinfectant. I picked up the basin. It was pitted and corroded, full of tiny pinprick-sized holes. Our whisky had eaten through the container in one night and was at work on the wooden floor! All our efforts had gone for naught. We had sacrificed three days' spud rations to clean and disinfect the area around our bunks! George did not appear to be consoled when I pointed out to him, "Better the wash-basin and the floor than our stomach lining," but he rather ruefully agreed with me.

When the Allies landed in Normandy in June of 1944, the inmates of Stalag Luft IV, near Gross Tychow, went wild with joy. If ever an occasion called for special celebration, this was it! Jerry was not about to issue a special ration of beer (which he had been known to do once before at Christmas). After all, it was only another futile Allied assault much like Dieppe, and scarcely worth getting excited about. They would all be pushed back into the sea. If the *gefangeners* wished to take it seriously and create a carnival atmosphere, that was their business. Our earlier disastrous attempts at distilling hard liquor had taught us to leave the dubious method requiring potatoes alone, and to concentrate on using jam or some other preserve which had a large sugar content. The still we used was quite elaborate and could be set up in a convenient location, usually a wash-room where there was running water on hand for use in the final step of the distillation process.

This operation was on a larger scale than our previous attempt and should enable all the men in hut 10A to raise a glass to toast the Allied landing in France. The fiery alcohol, when diluted in water to which some lemon extract had been added, was passable. What it lacked in subtlety was made up for in potency. The evening of June 6, 1944, was a memorable one for the happy men in hut 10A. The still worked far into the early morning hours spiking the glasses of lemon juice with a continuous flow of liquid fire as the men filed unsteadily past the brewmaster who was in charge of production. It was a glorious drunk as glass after glass was raised to our brave allies and countrymen who had made the assault on *Fortress Europa*. We drank to eventual victory, we drank to the souls of our comrades-in-arms whose torn and twisted flesh lay scattered on the beaches of Normandy, we drank to the wives and lovers of these brave men who were laying down their lives to wipe out ugliness and bestiality from tortured Europe, but most of all we drank to the promise of freedom which is never so cherished as it is by those who have lost it. We drank ourselves insensible and suffered, without exception, the following morning, from such hangovers as only unadulterated alcohol can cause. There was not a man among us who did not agree that it was a glorious celebration and worth every moment of the semi-paralysed penance which we were all required to pay the following day.

Our experiments with whisky-making and the distillation of dubious alcohol, while noteworthy enough, were small operations compared to the regular and steady production of what I shall describe, with a great deal of lenience, as a unique vintage of home-made wine. Since the main ingredient was water, to which some raisins and yeast had been added, it was quite readily available and was consumed on any suitable occasion such as a birthday or holiday celebration. It was very potent and, in spite of frequent filtering and decantings, remained cloudy and unattractive to the eye. It was sour to the palate with a bouquet rather resembling vomit. We bravely forced ourselves to consume it until the desired state of inebriation was achieved.

New Year's Eve of 1944 was our last occasion for serious wine consumption. The winter to follow was shortly to plunge us all into the final chaotic months of Germany's death agonies. In the forced marches which took place, we struggled for our very lives and for these reasons our last party will always remain unforgettable. It was as though we sensed the trials and hardships which we would shortly be forced to endure, and were therefore determined to make it special. That evening I achieved some special notoriety by earning the dubious distinction of being the first man in camp to throw up in 1945. For some reason my fellow prisoners found this highly amusing. I suppose it all depends on your perspective because to me it was far more hilarious when Willie Cowie lost everything into the night-latrine barrel - including his upper and lower dentures! It was a few days before he very gingerly allowed them inside his mouth again. Willie failed to see the humour, but it afforded the rest of us much laughter and the story was retold often with much relish and very little sympathy.

In retrospect, it becomes a source of wonder that so many ex-prisoners of war still survive so many years later when one pauses to consider the varieties of brew with which we experimented, subjecting our weakened digestive systems to all sorts of strange and untried mixtures. As young as we then were, it must inevitably follow, as night follows day, that many of us are today still, in some measure, paying for those Bacchanalian nights. There is a well-known aphorism which says that man is what he eats. If this applies with equal validity to what he drinks there must be indeed a motley collection of eccentric ex-prisoners of war abroad in this land today! It is perhaps just as well that they gather in one place only on rare occasions, and probably fortunate for them that in most cases they are subjected to the steadying and sobering influence of wives and families who keep a close rein on them.

CHAPTER THIRTEEN
Hunger March

Over the space of some forty-odd years, the details of prisoner-of-war events start to fade. Some events still retain their vivid and detailed clarity, while others begin to melt into themselves so that only the high points remain. This seems particularly true of the more unpleasant events of our years of captivity.

The forced marches across northern Europe endured by Allied prisoners of war from the many camps in East Prussia, occupied Poland and Germany are bitter memories to all who shared the experience. For most of us, with the possible exception of those who kept detailed diaries, the moment-to-moment events have all merged into an overall miasmic blur of privation and endurance. This is due mainly to reasons mentioned previously, namely one's tendency to forget the bad times and remember the better ones.

In a strange way too, the forced marches of the spring of 1945 gave us a sense of being part of the action again. We were back in the thick of it again, and no longer felt sidelined while momentous history was being made. The shared experiences which were to follow formed a basis for a lifetime of strong post-war association which time never seems to dim. In fact, the reverse appears to be the case as the ranks of ex-prisoners of war begin to thin out with the passing of time.

147

In the winter of 1944/45 the war was fast drawing to a close. Oncoming Russian forces were closing in on our camp which was situated in north-eastern Germany (or occupied Poland). It was scarcely six months since we had arrived in this camp near Gross Tychow.

Speculation about our fate was rather varied. Some of us were quite sure we would be moving again. Others felt Jerry would simply dash off and leave us to the advancing Red Army. But as hostages, we were valuable to our captors. However, there was virtually no way of moving us since the railways were desperately needed by the retreating German forces. One thing was certain. They had to make up their minds very soon. A glance at the map of northern Europe made it quite clear that unless they made a move we could be in for another evacuation by sea in a sort of little Dunkirk operation. This was not a pleasant prospect for those of us who remembered our recent journey from East Prussia.

One morning in early February of 1945 the axe, which had been hanging over our heads for most of the winter, finally fell. The senior NCO, Vic Clarke, prior to dismissing the morning parade made an announcement. "Gentlemen, I have been informed that by orders of the German high command this camp is to be vacated. We will be moving out in two day's time. Everyone is to be allowed to bring a change of clothes and an amount of food equivalent to one day's German rations plus the Red Cross food supplement which you can comfortably carry, as well as one army blanket each. I have also been informed that as no transportation is available we shall be carrying out this evacuation on foot. I have been given no information as to our eventual destination. In any case they very likely don't know themselves. That is all I have to say gentleman except to say good luck and God bless you all."

Prisoners of war on the march, winter of 1944/45. Sketch by Lee Kenyon first appeared in *The Camp*.

Now that the uncertainty of the past few weeks was over, a general air of relief prevailed. Although the prospect of a forced march in the dead of winter in northern Europe was not pleasant, we now knew at least what was ahead, and could plan accordingly. We were, to some small extent, in control of our fate, and could get down to making our plans for the march. Generally speaking, we were in reasonable shape, and had recently been issued with new American army boots which the Germans had acquired from somewhere. Most of us would be leaving something behind since the orders were quite plain; and, in any case, common sense dictated that no one was going to carry heavy books, or other useless items where our lives could depend on our ability to withstand the unknown trials and tests of endurance which lay ahead.

Our barracks, which up to now had been kept reasonably tidy, began to assume an aspect of chaos and confusion as each of us, absorbed in his own plans for survival, sorted out his pathetic belongings, and made decisions on what to take and what to leave behind. That which we decided to abandon was destroyed or torn up and tossed haphazardly aside to add to the growing piles of crockery, cardboard boxes, books, mementos, clothes, boots, sports equipment, kitbags, empty tins and wash-basins.

One of the difficult decisions concerned cigarettes. Many of us had some, and a few of us had accumulated several thousand in cartons sent from home from caring friends and relatives. They would be valuable in the weeks ahead, but bulky to carry. You could not reasonably ask a buddy to carry what you could not manage. In the end, however, very few were left behind. We had heard stories of deteriorating paper-money value in the countryside, so the decision to bring as many as we could with us would prove a sound one.

The morning of February 6, 1945, dawned frosty, but clear. It was to most Canadians what could be described as a perfect winter's day. We had been told that morning parade would be delayed until eleven o'clock, but that upon completion of roll-call we were to move off directly, so that what we carried on parade would be what we would carry out of the camp. The men began to assemble for this last parade. Those of us who had obeyed the letter of the law regarding personal belongings found some of the amazing sights almost impossible to believe. Some prisoners dragged hastily built sleds piled with equipment lashed on with bits of rope. Equipment which some considered absolutely indispensable included home-made blower fires, folding chairs, guitars, ice skates, footballs, kitchen equipment fashioned from empty tins, pillows, extra boots, basins and even heavy technical books. This was the camp which we had arrived at virtually empty-handed seven months previously! Captain Robert Scott, famed explorer of the South Pole, would have been impressed by the ingenuity displayed in the distribution of these incredible loads on the hastily built sleds. All that was missing was the noisy barking of Husky dogs, and the drivers' whips to control the prisoners who had harnessed themselves to these incredible contraptions.

We moved off around noon in no fixed order. The column of men was roughly three abreast, flanked on either side by German soldiers wearing the blue-grey *Luftwaffe* field uniforms, and carrying their rifles. The novelty of the situation gave an almost holiday atmosphere to the proceedings. Those with the heavily loaded sleds were having problems with shifting loads and sled runners which functioned reasonably well in the snow, but caused problems in areas where snow had blown away or melted into muddy refrozen pot-holes. The amused guards no doubt reflected on their good fortune in being part of such a loosely disciplined operation when they could have been part of a much larger, grimmer retreat which was taking place further east in Poland. From time to time we were halted and moved to the side of the road to allow German lorry loads of exhausted looking men to pass by, heading west, or other convoys of relatively fresh, young, scared-looking replacements heading towards the fighting and almost certain death or capture. Our guards had much to be thankful for, but then, most of them had already tasted action on the Eastern Front, and carried visible evidence of the grim reality of winter warfare on the Russian front. They no doubt breathed a silent heartfelt prayer of thanks to have survived their share of action on the terrible, frozen plains of Russia and eastern Europe.

In a war such as the one which was now reaching its climax, it was not often that the fighting men actually gazed at each other face to face. The killing was on such a large, almost impersonal, scale that the mere pressing of a button could wipe out hundreds of men and women and children. The enemy was rarely seen. The exchanges of eye contact between the evacuating prisoners and the German army soldiers contained no hatred in them. Somehow we knew, and they knew, that all of us were helpless pawns in a high-level struggle of idealogies. When the "enemy" is found to be a shivering half-starved fellow human, far from home and loved ones, the hatred melts and a feeling almost of mutual compassion and respect for each other replaces it. My own feelings could be summed up very easily. In spite of my desperate situation I would not have changed places with a single one of them. I could at least see a faint glimmer of light of a better life to follow. The German soldiers knew in their hearts that all was lost and their country was in ruins. The rebirth of Germany would take place, but just then nobody believed in miracles.

The bond which linked fighting men of opposite forces did not, however, exist between Allied airmen and German civilians. It was not evident at first, since we were in the northern farming territory which had remained relatively untouched by strategic bombing. But in the weeks to come, as we drew closer to the environs of Berlin, the attitude of German civilians became one of violently displayed hatred towards us. This was understandable, since most of them had lost homes and loved ones in the terrible air raids inflicted by both the Royal Air Force and the bombers of the United States Air Force. It was common knowledge in these final days of the war that downed Allied flyers stood a good chance of being lynched or badly injured by vigilantes if they were unfortunate enough to fall into their hands. In the days to come, we were to experience firsthand some of this hatred and feel thankful for the presence of armed German soldiers. Their prime function was to prevent our escape, but in many instances they were forced to use their rifles to keep the hostile crowds from attacking us with anything they could lay their hands on. For this reason, too, our march bypassed most of the larger towns and villages. Whenever possible we moved along back roads and country lanes. If passing through a town centre was unavoidable, we were usually sneaked through in the small hours of the morning in utter darkness. It was eerie to see the closed shutters of a sleeping town, and to experience the utter silence, broken only by the shuffle of hundreds of plodding prisoners' feet. I had had a similar experience when marching through the blacked-out streets of Uxbridge when I had first arrived in England. It had been rather eerie then, as well, but not like this when we knew only too well that our lives could depend on getting through the town or village without attracting too much attention.

The first few days of the march were, as I mentioned previously, almost enjoyable. The weather was cold, but dry. Our food supplies were as good as they would ever be, since we had left the camp with close to a week's issue of Red Cross parcels containing chocolate, jam, biscuits and tinned meats. We were averaging about twenty to twenty-five kilometres a day and bedding down at night in the relative warmth of the hay in the barns of commandeered farms in the countryside.

The day would begin around 7 am when German sentries would bang on the barn-doors with rifle butts and awaken us with the usual "Raus, raus, alles raus fur appel." It took us little time to fall in for morning head count since we slept fully clothed. Those of us who felt the need to wash and shave did so after parade, in cold water from a pump. For those of us who considered a morning wash and shave unnecessary, all that was required was a quick run-through of the hair to brush stray bits of straw out and we were ready to face the day.

When the guards had satisfied themselves that they had lost no one overnight, we were dismissed for about an hour and a half to eat breakfast and to prepare ourselves for the day's march. The aroma of ersatz coffee announced the issue of our German ration of coffee and black bread. The coffee, although barely drinkable, was hot and felt good, and could be used for shaving by those of us who balked at shaving in cold water.

The first hour or so of the day's march was usually the most unpleasant, until the stiffness of our joints wore off. The penetrating cold of the unheated barns, even in the relative warmth of the straw, made our muscles and joints complain and, in addition, the new boots which we were breaking in had resulted in sore feet and blisters which went untreated. Every hour we were given a ten-minute rest which, although welcome, made it difficult to get started once we had cooled off somewhat. The first few steps were agonizing until we again settled into the monotonous rhythm of the relentless move westward. At noon a longer halt was called and we rested by the roadside. Some of the prisoners carved off a slice of German black bread and spread jam or tinned meat on it for lunch. Most of us were too tired to bother and stretched out as best we could until the trek was, all too soon, resumed.

During this march my messing buddy was a New Zealand army private, whose real name was Ernie Petherick, but who had assumed the identity of a Canadian pilot named Frank Shorrock. He was commonly referred to as Tank. Tank was one of the last few army privates to remain undetected by German security personnel. We had been messing together since the fall of 1942 when my previous army buddy swap-over, George Stamp, had been discovered, and returned to the British army via a three-week rest in the camp cooler for having the temerity to impersonate a Canadian flyer. Tank had been swept up by the German army during the invasion of Crete.

154

He had survived the shocking conditions of the Salonica death camp and had ended up in Germany itself. He was actually a Canadian who had gone to New Zealand during the Depression days prior to the war to try his luck, eventually enlisting in the New Zealand army.

As his name implied, Tank was a big teddy bear of a man who burned calories on a much larger scale than the average prisoner of war. He suffered from the reduced rations more than most of us due to his enormous size, but never took more than his fair share. He was always cheerful, and a tremendous boost to our sometimes low morale. He had one other attribute which did much to endear him to those who knew him. Due to his size and high metabolism he radiated heat, and those of us who were fortunate enough to sleep near him in our straw accommodations were grateful for his body warmth. Picture this mountain of a man surrounded by shivering men "sneaking a warm." If you have ever seen a large sow surrounded by greedy little piglets seeking nourishment and warmth, you have the idea.

Back on the march, the late afternoon found the ragged columns of prisoners suffering from lack of food and looking forward with longing to the end of the day and a brief respite from the weather. By this time, quite a few had dropped out of the column and been picked up by the army lorry which followed us. There was room for forty men who could not keep up. It was definitely a last resort type of thing since, once aboard the truck and no longer moving one's limbs, frost-bite was an ever present and very real danger. On many nights our sleep was disturbed by the moans of prisoners who suffered from the agony of slowly returning circulation to frost-bitten feet.

The most urgent requirement, once we had come to the end of our day's march, was a hot meal. An issue of hot soup by the Germans, although welcome, did little to satisfy since it was watery and devoid of nourishment. If the occasional issue of soup had any meat, it was horse meat and barely edible. It was an effort to prepare any food. In any case open fires were not permitted for security reasons. Although the Royal Air Force had been alerted to the fact that there were many prisoners of war marching across Europe, there was no guarantee that fires burning in the countryside would not draw their fire. For this reason our meal, such as it was, was eaten cold. It was generally a slice of spam or bully beef on a slab of black bread. Later on when our Red Cross issue became depleted, our evening meal consisted of the watery soup and one or two boiled potatoes eaten in their jackets. It would have been unthinkable to waste valuable food energy by peeling them.

With our evening meal, such as it was, inside us, most of the prisoners were ready to hit the hay, both literally and figuratively. A few hardy souls made contact with French or Polish internees to swap belongings such as watches, extra boots or cigarettes for the odd chicken or new-laid egg. Since darkness fell early in northern Europe in mid-February, there was very little sign of life by seven thirty or eight o'clock. The long night silence was broken only by snoring, quiet conversation or the whimpers of frost-bite sufferers.

In this manner we slowly made our way across north-eastern Germany and eventually crossed the Oder River south of Stettin. We were now heading in a north-westerly direction. As the condition of the prisoners began to deteriorate further, the Germans began resting us occasionally for a complete day to allow us to recover somewhat from the gruelling ordeal. At morning roll-call, at one of these rest stops, an ominous announcement was made by the major to the assembled men.

"I have to inform you that tomorrow morning we will be on the road by seven o'clock and that the day's march will cover forty-two kilometres. No one will be permitted to fall behind. I advise you all to get a good night's sleep and be ready to march by 7 am. It is absolutely essential that we make our objective by tomorrow evening." We were told nothing more. However, a glance at the tattered maps some of us carried showed that we were getting close to the coast, as we worked our way along the ever widening estuary of the Oder River which emptied into the Pomeranian Bay. If you glance at a map of Germany, the town of Peenemünde, which we now know was the site of German rocket research, sits on a peninsula jutting out into the bay. Obviously this was the reason for the German concern to get us out of the area as quickly as possible. They were taking no chances on the possibility of suicide sabotage attempts by those among us who may not be genuine prisoners of war, but rather desperate Allied agents with orders to infiltrate the complex and plant explosives.

I can remember seeing the trails of what I now know to have been German test rockets being fired. But at the time none of us had any idea that we were witnessing the early days of rocket travel, as the German scientists perfected the terrible V2 rockets which were hitting London with such devastating effect.

Of the next day's march there is not much that stands out other than the memory of long hours of steady plodding. Surprisingly, we bore up rather well. It was the night that followed that was more draining on our strength and morale than the actual forced march. The combined effects of the strain of the march and the night that followed took their toll on our condition, and marked the beginning of a steady decline in our health. At the end of the long ordeal we found ourselves in a large open snow-covered plain. There were approximately five hundred men, plus the guards, for whom some kind of accommodation had to be found, but there were no farms in sight where we could expect to find a night's refuge from the elements. Now that we were in the heart of war-ravaged Germany, it was probably a good deal more difficult to commandeer farm buildings to shelter enemy prisoners. Whatever the reason, it became evident that we were expected to pass the night in the open fields.

The temperature was well below freezing. If we were to survive, it would be essential to build fires. The German major made his decision, which was for this night only to abandon black-out security and to permit fires. It was a humane act on his part, since he was at risk, too, if our camp-fires attracted the attention of the RAF. The long night that followed would be an experience none of us would forget. While the camp-fires provided warmth, they also had the effect of melting the snow and turning the frozen earth into wet mud. There was no place to lie where one could prevent the dampness from seeping through into our tired bones. We spent the entire night huddled as close to the fires as possible, using each other to prop ourselves up, and occasionally nodding off and waking up with a start as we shifted out of position.

The cold and damp penetrated deeper into my body as the long hours wore on, and as the sun rose the following morning there was not one of us who did not dread the prospect of another long march. Tired, hungry and half-frozen, with our morale drooping badly, we prepared to move off the following morning.

But for most of us, the lack of proper diet combined with the struggle to keep going was beginning to have its effect, and our health worsened accordingly. Dysentery weakened and dehydrated almost all of us, leaving us worn out and vulnerable to other ailments. The lack of facilities to maintain basic hygiene made it almost impossible to prevent lice from building up on our clothes and bodies. The ordeal of stripping and washing under a cold farm pump, unpleasant as it was in the winter temperatures, was the only alternative to accepting the disgusting vermin as a part of our existence. There were no medical supplies to ease the torment of the lice and crabs which crawled on us or to treat the gut-wrenching dysentery which got progressively worse.

The daily march was becoming a problem for the German authorities since they were finding it difficult to make arrangements for our overnight accommodation when they could not guarantee to get the slowly plodding prisoners to the commandeered farms by nightfall. In spite of their continued proddings and urgings to keep moving, most of the men responded by refusing to get up when our short rests were over. In any case, the guards themselves were not much better off since most of them were past military age or unfit for front-line duty.

One evening, as we were preparing to bed down, Tank asked me if I would like a bit of a break from routine the following day. He had been asked to be part of an advance party of two prisoners and a German officer and guard to go ahead of the column to search for overnight billets for the five hundred men of the main group. It would mean rising at five o'clock instead of seven and staying three or four hours ahead of the men until we arrived at whatever farm could be found to put us up for the night. Although I was ill, and suffering badly from cramps and dysentery, I jumped at the chance to move ahead of the column. The change might take our minds off the grim reality of the mass of suffering, complaining men which was helping to drag each of us down. A pleasant walk in the country with only three other humans for company might be a nice change. Besides, we would not bypass the larger village which lay in our path, but be routed through it by the two Germans who would be able to keep any unfriendly locals away from us since there were only two of us to protect. We might even stop for a beer at a convenient country inn!

The following day was a memorable one, and the one bright spot which relieved the drabness and suffering of the days past and those which were to follow. My German was then sufficient to carry on halting conversation and we found our German *oberleutnant* and corporal to be decent sorts who genuinely felt compassion for our plight, and who wished as fervently as we did that it would all be over soon. Old battered photographs were dragged out and each of us made suitable comments about our respective wives and sweethearts. The biggest treat of all was reserved for early afternoon when we had booked reservations for the men at a rather prosperous-looking farm.

Most German farms were what are usually described as mixed farms, growing potatoes and vegetables, and sometimes maintaining several scraggy looking chickens or a few pigs. This one had, in addition, a dozen dairy cows. Probably because this farmer lived in a part of Germany which had been relatively untouched by the war, he was a friendly sort, and appeared eager to co-operate with the *oberleutnant*. We had arrived at milking time and the pails of fresh milk were the first we had seen in nearly four years. Our fascination with the brimming buckets must have been obvious because the farmer dipped a large ladle into one of them and thrust it towards us with an unmistakable gesture to help ourselves.

It was rich and creamy and had cooled to a delicious freshness. With many a "Danke schön" we drank deeply and

160

appreciatively of its white frothy goodness. Both of us were aware that its unaccustomed richness would probably be too much for our shrunken stomachs and upset digestive systems. We drank slowly and deeply and with reckless unconcern for the after-effects. We paid later for our abandon with severe cramps and nausea, but agreed it had been worth it.

We had been on the road for over a month and had moved well into Germany. The skies overhead were almost constantly alive with aircraft. By daylight the squadrons of American bombers were visible and flew in large formations which glinted in the sun as they flew overhead. At night we listened to the throbbing of hundreds of RAF bombers delivering their deadly loads, and felt the earth tremble as the bombs exploded on nearby targets. Occasionally Lockheed Lightnings flashed overhead and we watched with growing apprehension as these twin-boomed fighter-bombers searched for anything that moved.

It had to happen. In one of those unfortunate, but almost unavoidable tragedies of war, we were hit by the murderous strafing fire of a single, low-flying Lightning which seemed to come, literally, out of nowhere. It lasted only a few seconds. With a screaming roar and with little warning it was upon us. There was time to dive into the ditches which ran along each side of the dusty road, to watch with horrified disbelief as the deadly cannon turned the road-bed into exploding fountains of debris and dust. Then silence. In the aftermath there was no anger, but we had not escaped unhurt. There were casualties, and tragically, one death. One of the English prisoners had received a cannon shell in his chest and died instantly. The wounded men - all prisoners - were given emergency treatment by the guards and taken by army truck to a hospital nearby. If the American pilot ever discovered when he was debriefed that one of his targets had been a column of Allied

161

prisoners of war he must have indeed found it difficult to sleep. Unfortunately, in wartime when forces are advancing rapidly, this type of thing does occur more often than many people realize. For those of us who escaped unhurt it was a shattering experience, and a reminder, if one were needed, that we were well within range of British and American attacking aircraft. For the next day or so the mere sight of marauding Lightnings was sufficient cause to take immediate cover until the danger of strafing was past.

A point had now been reached where a difficult decision had to be made. It had become obvious that I was approaching the point where I would be unable to keep up with the column. It was clear that I was becoming too weak to continue unless some adequate treatment was received for the dysentery which was making it impossible to sleep. Rest was essential if one was to be able to continue. Extra rations, too, would be necessary if I was to regain my declining strength. I had taken to swallowing large quantities of charcoal which was supposed to have a binding effect. Some of us got some relief, but for me nothing seemed to help. Perhaps if I could exchange my wrist-watch for extra bread it might help. The crystal had fallen out and was being held in place by strips of adhesive bandage but it still kept reasonably accurate time. I gave it to Tank to flog for whatever he could get for it. Since it did not look too attractive with the dirty strips of Band Aid holding the crystal in place I instructed Tank to remove the sticky tape, and be careful to hold the watch face up during negotiations with any prospective purchaser. It would be rather embarrassing if the face should fall out when it was handed over to a local German for an agreed amount of black bread. Most German civilians were anxious to get hold of any watch that worked, and Tank had little trouble finding someone who agreed to buy it in exchange for four loaves of bread. We stuffed some of the dry bread into us and hoped by the following day to find some improvement. The pangs of hunger were eased by the stodgy bread, heavily fortified with sawdust. For a day or so our stomachs did have something to work on, and some of my strength returned, but the ever present dysentery continued without let up. I was having difficulty as well with badly blistered feet which, for me, was unusual, since I have seldom been bothered by breaking in new boots or shoes. No doubt the constant wetness had caused my skin to soften and blister. I was certainly not alone in this. We all hobbled along like old men whose joints were near to seizing up.

For those who could not keep up with the slowly moving prisoners there was one alternative. Periodically the Germans were allowing those who could not continue to be picked up by truck and delivered to nearby farms for a few days rest. They took no responsibility for the prisoners who took advantage of this since they could spare few guards from the main column to accompany us.

In mid-March I made up my mind to drop out and take my chances in one of these "rest camps" as they were known. I would be part of the next load of sick men, but on no account would I ride the truck. I had seen the effects of frost-bite on those who allowed their limbs to remain inactive for too long. It was indeed a difficult decision to make, since Tank and I had been through so much together in the last two or three years. We shook hands slowly on the road, amid the bleak countryside, and a slanting wind blew flakes of spring snow across the track of the men who moved slowly out of sight. Tank turned and waved and gave a thumbs up which I returned and then moved off at right angles along a side-road with the twenty or so men who had chosen to take their chances away from the relative security of the main body of prisoners.

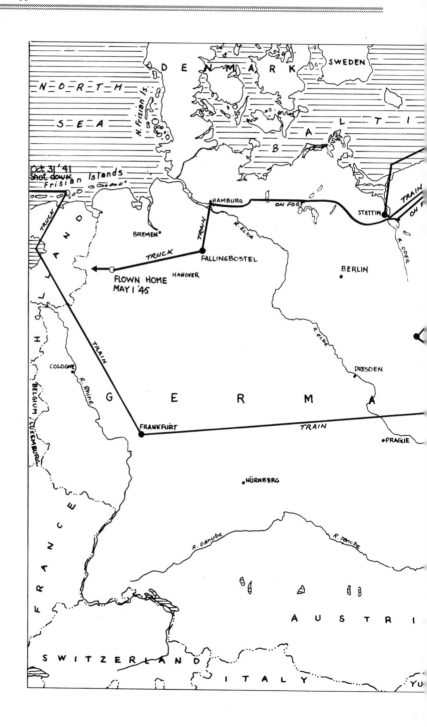

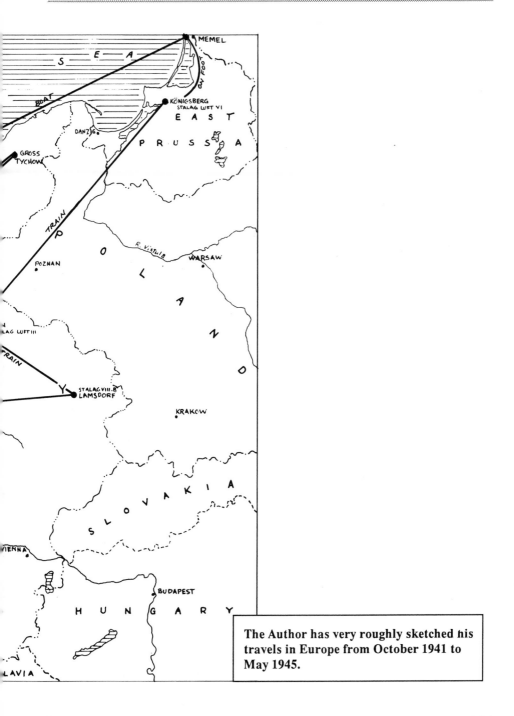

The Author has very roughly sketched his
travels in Europe from October 1941 to
May 1945.

The farm where we found ourselves was little different from the others we had seen on our trek across Europe. At least we could look forward to a few days' respite from the endless marching and seek the security and warmth of the barns which sheltered us from the weather. My spare shirt followed my watch, this time for a cooked chicken which I shared with a fellow prisoner who had made the contact. We slowly munched on this fresh meat and decided that the shirt had been well spent.

On the first sunny day we had a good clean-up. In the warm sun the freezing cold water of the pump was easier to endure, and my clothes dried quickly in the sun while I lounged around in my faithful blanket and speculated on our fate. The two guards had no idea of our next move and merely shrugged their shoulders when the subject was brought up. We accepted this and resigned ourselves to taking it a day at a time. We were, after all, more or less secure from any marauding Allied aircraft who did not consider innocent-looking farm buildings to be worthy of attack.

In the next few days most of us recovered some of our strength. By bartering our personal belongings, or our valuable cigarettes which some still carried, it was possible to supplement the regulation German issue of bread and potatoes. The chicken which I had eaten had helped significantly to restore some strength and spirit. There were one or two incidents, however, which did much to make one wonder about the human instinct for survival when man is reduced to the bare essentials of existence, namely shelter and sustenance.

Most of the farm labourers encountered were not German but civilian internees of countries which had been overrun by Germany. The bartering which took place between Allied

166

prisoners of war and internees was usually carried out in French, since there were many French nationals held by Germany. I am sorry to say they were not above taking advantage of our unfortunate situation and were quite often successful in outwitting their so-called allies. When a tin of fifty cigarettes was exchanged for a similarly sized tin of sugar, we soon found out that unless the product was examined before the deal was completed, it very often turned out to be a half-inch layer of sugar covering a tin of sand. The only defence I can offer for this kind of despicable behaviour is that these men had had to become accomplished in the art of survival through their years in Germany. They had been reduced to the state of every man for himself where deprivation and need very often drives desperate men. These are trivial incidents in the light of what we see and hear almost daily on television and in newspapers, but they did have an effect on me and will always tarnish the memories of the acts of heroism and unselfishness of which that same human animal is capable in wartime.

The temporary respite from the long march we had endured was most welcome. True, conditions were less than idyllic, and our weakened condition left most of us in no fit state to do very much other than rest or sun ourselves, but it was a pleasant enough way to pass the time. After a week or so of relative relaxation we were not surprised, nor indeed too upset, when we were told we were to be on the move again, particularly since we were to be moved by rail to a large camp near Fallingbostel, south and west of Hamburg. It was not to be a long trip, but could prove to be interesting. Our route would take us directly through the city of Hamburg. From the narrow slits in the boxcar, we were able to glimpse the devastation which constant raids by Allied aircraft had wrought. The sight is impossible to describe. I remember an American flyer of German extraction gazing at the miles of rubble which extended as far as one could see in every direction. Tears streamed from his eyes as he saw the desolation of this tortured city in the land of his forebears. And yet somehow life continued amid the ruins. Our train pulled up in the dock area of the Elbe River alongside a German cruiser which was being efficiently serviced by dock workers. As we did so the air-raid warning sounded, and in full daylight American bombers pounded the very dock area in which our train was drawn up. Amid the falling bombs we gazed helplessly and fearfully from our front-row seats at the battle. The German cruiser was the target and was not going to suffer without a fight. The concussion of the anti-aircraft guns was punctuated by the explosion of the near misses as bombs rained down all around us. The main reason for our fear was the feeling of helplessness we felt at being locked in boxcars, unable to take shelter from the fight. At the first alarm our guards had hastily withdrawn, leaving us to sweat it out. The bedlam was not without an element of humour. As I attempted to light a cigarette for myself and for a fellow prisoner my hand shook, and the hand which he offered, trying to steady mine, was shaking badly too. With great difficulty the two of us managed to make cigarette and lighter flame contact and we laughed together grimly at the terror which had gripped us. Once again the act of lighting up would help to ease the tension as it had done before on our trip from East Prussia through the Baltic Sea.

This time, however, we were to escape unscathed. Except for the damage to our morale, we were unhurt. The German cruiser, too, appeared not to have suffered any damage. It was a long time before we began to move again. No doubt the railway lines had been damaged in the raid and would have to be repaired before our journey could be resumed. Another night came and went before we felt a jolt from a locomotive hitching on and we began to move.

168

Fallingbostel was not far from Hamburg and our trip was to come to its end as we drew up slowly in the freight yards of this small town. It was good to be freed of the cramped quarters of the boxcars as we moved again by foot to the camp which could be seen from the railway siding where we had been unloaded.

As we marched into the camp itself we were greeted by fellow prisoners whom we had not seen for some time and who, by all evidence, had not been having an easy time of it. As tired and hungry as we were, we could not help but feel for these men who had been existing on starvation rations. Our ordeal, as bad as it had been, was no worse than the one endured by these half-starved men, and the conditions under which they had been surviving were about to be shared by all of us. Only one thing was certain. The Germans were in the final days of their death agonies and the end could not be far off.

CHAPTER FOURTEEN
A Most Memorable Meal

Few among us would have any trouble whatsoever in remembering and describing a truly memorable meal. We have all enjoyed this pleasurable experience at one time or another, when a particular occasion has called for a celebration: a wedding anniversary, your first meal with your loved one in your new home, a particular restaurant where food, atmosphere, service and pleasant company have combined to make the occurrence unforgettable. Perhaps you have prepared a particularly successful gourmet meal with candle-light and wine and everything has gone perfectly. There are many circumstances which make a meal special.

Some years ago Pierre Berton held a contest in *The Toronto Star* in which contestants were requested to describe their most memorable meal. Those which he felt were the best or most interesting were later published, in part, in his daily column and the winners received an autographed copy of one of his latest books. The meal I am going to describe was prepared in the closing days of the war amidst the sound of battle as the British army was thundering in pursuit of German forces. We, as freshly liberated prisoners of war, had been left to fend for ourselves, since our German guards had joined the fast-fleeing forces of the Third Reich.

It was a simple meal, yet made all the more memorable by the conditions under which it came about. My description of it was judged worthy of publication and I received an appropriately autographed copy of Berton's book. With much pleasure, I re-create this meal for you now.

It was April 1945, and our long march had been completed in the winter months under terrible conditions. Red Cross parcels had long since stopped coming to us. We had been marched so far west that it now became obvious to the guards that in order to hang on to us we had to turn around and march east again.

I was very weak and had decided that at all costs I would have to find a way of defecting from this second march. I reasoned that if I could be at the rear of the column, we stood a good chance of being cut off by the fast approaching Eighth Army forces. This is in fact what happened, for we had covered only twenty miles or so when we were informed that we were returning to the camp to await instructions.

A few days later we were in a frenzy of joy and delight as British and Canadian forces liberated our camp. Deliriously happy ex-prisoners of war swarmed over the countryside, savouring their sudden, new-found freedom and generally getting in the way of the advancing army. So much so, in fact, that Field Marshall, Sir Bernard Montgomery was obliged to make a personal appeal to us to restrain ourselves, and attempt to be patient if we possibly could. He told us that arrangements were in progress to fly us to England as soon as possible. Meanwhile the British tanks and trucks streamed past our camp and received a tumultuous greeting from the *kriegies*. Smiling Tommys sat on the tanks tossing bread and treats to the half-starved men as they roared past. As I stood by the road waving to the battle-hardened men, a British soldier tossed me an entire loaf of freshly baked white bread!

For nearly four years I had not seen such a luxury! The bread was soft inside, yet crusty. The aroma was delectable and overwhelmingly reminiscent of pre-war bakery shop delights which, until now, had existed only on the outer fringes of our imaginations, discussed reverently with other prisoners of war in endless conversation where food was the favourite topic.

My immediate reaction was to sit down then and scoff the lot in an orgy of gratification which would probably have resulted in an immediate wave of protest from a shrunken stomach unused to such a luxury. No, a better idea would be to build a fire and toast it slice by slice. I needed fresh butter. In the bottom of my kit-bag, reserved for emergency, I carried an unopened tin of fifty Gold Flake cigarettes. Cigarettes were the only currency with any real value both in prison camp and in the countryside. German marks were virtually worthless at this stage of the war. We were situated in an area composed mainly of farms. The farmers kept livestock and poultry and were willing to sell to anyone with the necessary purchasing power. Livestock meant milk and butter, and poultry meant eggs. Armed with my precious tin of Gold Flakes I set out to barter for groceries and approached a farm similar to the many farms I had become so familiar with in our march across Poland and Germany. There was a man loading a wagon with manure, who looked up as I approached. I tried out my German on him and showed him my cigarettes. He turned out to be a Frenchman who was working as a labourer. Although free to leave, he was playing it safe by remaining on the farm where he was sure of eating, but was willing to trade some butter and some eggs for a suitable sum. The transaction was quickly completed and I headed back to camp with enough butter for my bread and one dozen freshly laid brown farm eggs nestling in straw in a paper bag! With difficulty I controlled my impatience. The stubborn dysentery, which no amount of medicine could alleviate and which plagued me

173

My darling Jeyune,

So much has happened since I last wrote that I hardly know where to begin.

We were liberated by the "desert rats" three days ago. You have no idea of the scenes which took place. It is a day I shall remember as long as I live. For five days we had heard the gunfire, and then the tanks rolled into the camp and we all went crazy.

I expect to leave here and be flown back to England in about three days time, dear, so with luck I may be there by Sunday night. There is so much chaos that it is quite possible we may

be delayed.

It seems hardly possible that I shall be seeing you again before another week is out. I am so impatient to be back that I can't sit still, or concentrate, or eat. This letter will probably seem disconnected and won't make much sense, but you'll just have to excuse it, darling.

We were only allowed one letter, so could you tell my folks that I'm on my way. They will most likely be informed by the ministry but I don't want them to think I've forgotten them.

The army boys who liberated us have been very good to us. Yesterday I had my first white bread for 3½ years. We

April 19

endlessly, was about to receive the finest treatment. No art collector delicately transporting fragile fine china, no mother gently bathing an infant for the first time, or alchemist pouring molten gold from beaker to beaker ever exhibited the care and gentleness that I bestowed on my precious bundle of eggs as I made my way back to camp.

My preparations were slow and deliberate in spite of the excitement which I could feel building as the juices began to flow in anticipation of the feast! The roof of my mouth actually ached. My fire glowed cosily and I set my billycan

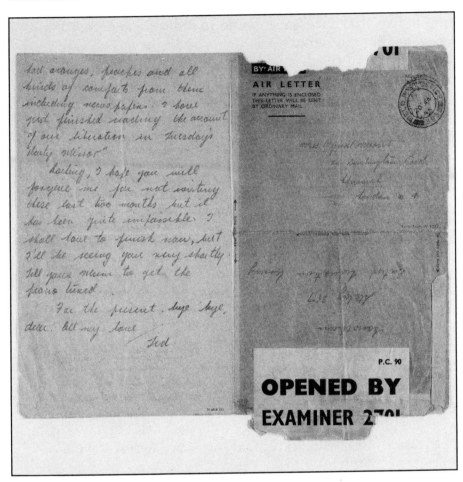

Letter written after liberation, April 1945.

gently in place and slowly and with infinite care gently cracked
one egg and allowed its contents to slip into the simmering
water. I cracked another and repeated the process again and
again. I gently freed the gold and white goodness of each
successive egg until all twelve were immersed in the boiling
water. An exquisite gossamer froth bobbed tantalizingly on the
surface of the steaming water as I set the billycan slightly to
one side. With great care I took the crusty loaf of bread and
sawed off a thickish slice with my jack-knife, allowing the

fragrant aroma of the fresh bread to seduce and enravish me, knowing that the unbearable agony of desire was soon to be gratified and fulfilled as no yearning lovers had ever been. I carefully sliced off five more slices putting half of the loaf to one side. One by one I toasted them and gazed in reverence as the white bread slowly browned to an amber loveliness, with a border of darker crust like the mahogany frame surrounding a Van Gogh interpretation of sunlight. The butter I allowed to soften from the heat of the fire until it became almost liquid. There was to be no tearing of the texture by awkward trembling hands attempting to spread the butter. The golden richness of the melted butter would be lovingly applied and allowed to impregnate each slice with its sweet fragrance. All was now in readiness for the orgy of self-indulgence. The delicately poached eggs were carefully lifted from the billycan and set gently down, two to each slice, on the crisp warm toast. I didn't care that my plate was not of the finest Doulton china, but was in fact a hastily scraped piece of wood. There was no table spread with snowy white linen. My crude wooden platter merely rested across my lap. I possessed no cutlery, only a worn and tarnished metal spoon, but I challenge any gourmet who has dined well of rare and exotic delicacies in any corner of the earth to say that any meal was more well received.

The next hour passed in a transport of ecstasy as I slowly finished off the entire lot, with occasional pauses for a smoke to permit it to settle. I was not about to risk being violently ill and thereby lose the soothing balm which the softly poached eggs were affording to my tortured guts. I could actually sense the healing power of good diet at work. As the afternoon wore on, I allowed the drowsiness which invariably accompanies gastronomic satisfaction to take over and gently snoozed with what must have been a smile of contentment on my face.

There was, in this particular instance, no question of sharing. This may appear strange to the reader. Over the previous four years of captivity it would have been unthinkable not to have done so. Our whole code of existence was based on mutual trust and equal sharing of our meagre resources. This was different. In a very real sense it was each man for himself, though not in an unkind, selfish way. We were each free to exploit our new-found freedom and even wealth, since cigarettes made some of us wealthy. I chose to do it this way. Other former prisoners bartered for cameras and binoculars or various other souvenirs and have probably to this day got old German bayonets, swastikas or what have you gathering dust in some forgotten place. However, I will always have my memory of that never-to-be-forgotten meal, enjoyed that afternoon in Germany while the chaos and urgency of war raged unheeded around me.

CHAPTER FIFTEEN
Flight to Freedom

In the days which followed, the euphoria of our newly acquired liberation dissipated quickly. It was replaced by an all-consuming desire to return to England and eventually to our native lands.

Although the odious black Swastika no longer flew over us, and the glorious Union Jack fluttered majestically in its place, the soil under our feet was foreign still. We all longed to shake the hated dust from our feet and tread once again in a free land.

The logistics involved in returning newly released prisoners of war added to the many problems which the liberating armies of the Allies had to deal with. We knew this, of course, and would be forever grateful to the men of the Eighth Army under the command of Field Marshall Montgomery for our release from captivity. However, it is impossible to describe the overwhelming urgency of our desire to return to our loved ones, to be in some measure responsible for our actions and decisions, to experience once again the dreams and aspirations which we knew to be a part of normal life.

I felt apprehensive about the prospect of being free once again. After three and a half years how would I cope when forced to deal once again with handling money, buying train

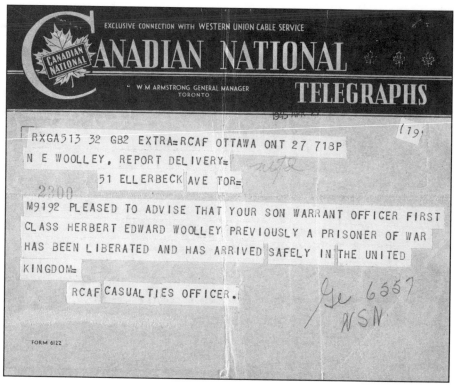

EXCLUSIVE CONNECTION WITH WESTERN UNION CABLE SERVICE

CANADIAN NATIONAL TELEGRAPHS

W M ARMSTRONG GENERAL MANAGER
TORONTO

RXGA513 32 GB2 EXTRA=RCAF OTTAWA ONT 27 718P

N E WOOLLEY, REPORT DELIVERY=

51 ELLERBECK AVE TOR=

M9192 PLEASED TO ADVISE THAT YOUR SON WARRANT OFFICER FIRST
CLASS HERBERT EDWARD WOOLLEY PREVIOUSLY A PRISONER OF WAR
HAS BEEN LIBERATED AND HAS ARRIVED SAFELY IN THE UNITED
KINGDOM=

RCAF CASUALTIES OFFICER.

FORM 6122

Telegram received by the author's parents upon his liberation, April 1945.

tickets, ordering a meal in a restaurant, conversing with members of the opposite sex? The prospect was terrifying! Like a chrysalis emerging from its cocoon and blinded by the light, I would surely grope ineffectively in simple situations.

Nevertheless the tantalizing prospect of true freedom overrode everything and obliterated any negative thoughts. Nothing on this earth can compare with the re-attainment of lost freedom. Without it all the pleasures that this world offers are as dry dust. It was almost within our grasp!

A fleet of DC3 aircraft was to fly from sunrise to sunset from any landing strip which could accommodate them. All prisoners would henceforth remember these ancient Dakotas with fondness. The thousands of assembled prisoners were loaded and dispatched to England as fast as the aircraft could land, load and take off. We merely moved by truck to the airfield and joined the long line of ex-prisoners which slowly moved forward as the men were loaded aboard.

Towards sundown those of us who had moved close to the head of the line were seized with a dreadful uncertainty. There was only sufficient daylight remaining for two or three aircraft to land, load, take off and return before darkness closed down repatriation operations until the following morning. After three and a half years, surely one more night in Nazi Germany was neither here nor there. Not so! Even today, forty-three years later, I cannot forget the feelings of utter disappointment and desolation that engulfed me as I saw the last aircraft take off for the day, and realized that my longing to be free of this country would have to go unrealized until the next day.

We climbed dejectedly back into the lorries which had transported us to the airfield and allowed ourselves to be driven back to the holding area to spend another endless night where sleep was out of the question. Only one thing concerned us: would the weather co-operate and permit flying to resume the following day. We did have one thing going in our favour. Those who had moved to the front of the queue would not lose their place and would be among the first to go on the following day.

The morning dawned fresh, clear and full of promise - perfect flying weather! We were loaded once again into the army trucks for the short ride to the landing strip near the Aller River. As the lorry drew within sight of the airfield, we could plainly see that two or three Dakotas had already touched down and were parked on the apron awaiting their cargo.

There was now no doubt that this was to be the last day of our long ordeal. Lunch in England was the glorious prospect which awaited us! The truck drew up beside an awaiting aircraft. A smiling flying officer with bright pilot's wings on his left breast greeted us with respectful courtesy. How young he looked! What must we have looked like to him and his crew as we clambered aboard in our motley collection of khaki uniforms which had been issued to us to replace our vermin-infested remnants of air force blue. Worn out as we were, many of us ill, disillusioned and unprepossessing, we felt almost ashamed to be in the presence of such smartly dressed airmen; and yet all of us were touched by the genuine respect which showed in the eyes of our liberators. Could they see beyond the unkempt appearance we presented, the deeply etched grime in the lines which creased our faces, the broken and dirty finger-nails, the hollow eyes and uncertainty and hesitancy of manner?

"Come on lads! Let's put on a show for these young sprogs!" someone shouted as we moved to the front of the line and prepared to board the aircraft. We formed up smartly in threes, threw back our shoulders and marched proudly in perfect step to the awaiting Dakota, and drew up with a perfectly executed halt. The crew of the aircraft snapped to attention, saluting smartly as we boarded. No one had issued a single command. It had been totally spontaneous and very moving, without a hint of embarrassment or self-consciousness.

The aircraft doors were closed with a bang, and it began its taxi to the end of the runway for take-off. The flight would take about two and a half hours: no stewardesses with hot meals, no in-flight movie, no seats which reclined. We merely sat on portable benches which had been secured to the floor along the length of the aircraft. Those who could see out through a small window kept their eyes peeled for the first sight of the shores of England. Each of us in turn moved to the

RAF ex-POW reunion in Abingdon, England, 1987.

window to view the emerging outline of the coast, and kept his thoughts to himself as he returned to his seat to await the touchdown at Northholt aerodrome on the fringe of London.

The Dakota landed and rolled to a stop; the hatch was opened and stairs drawn up to the opening. Brilliant sunshine streamed into the interior. What followed on the rest of that day has become a confused blur of swiftly occurring events.

I remember the smiling face of a uniformed WAAF who greeted me at the foot of the stairs leading from the hatch. There was one for each of us! I remember being relieved of my few rather pathetic belongings by my lady escort. Two efficient orderlies with giant-sized delousing guns approached. Zap, zap! Down my neck, up my sleeves, down my trousers, I was enveloped from head to toe in a white mist of insecticide powder. My arm was once again gently taken by my charming escort and we walked to a marquee tent where tables and benches were arranged. A lunch of tea and plates of sandwiches under a gay marquee tent awaited us in the sunshine of that April day in England.

My feelings that day are difficult to describe. As grim as it had been, I carried with me memories of friendships made, and experiences shared. Under that brightly coloured tent, surrounded by smiling WAAFs, I felt the first stirrings of the strong bond which existed between me and these men with whom I had endured so much. We had shared the intimate details of our lives. We had known each other's strength and weakness. I had seen tenderness and compassion displayed. I had seen the tears of deeply depressed souls, and witnessed the profound understanding of the strong amongst us comforting fellow prisoners in the depths of their misery.

On that April day in England my life lay ahead of me. I was to find peace and happiness to compensate for those years of hardship and privation. And in the years to come the close ties with former comrades would be maintained. Prisoner-of-war reunions would be occasions for remembering the positive aspects of those days we shared so long ago. As our ranks begin to diminish with the passing years, these bonds become ever stronger, as does my conviction that I have seen man at his finest - and I find comfort and hope for the future in this knowledge.

- The Beginning -

About the Author

Herbert E. (Ted) Woolley was born in Montreal, Quebec in 1921. He received his high school education in Lachine, Quebec. Shortly after graduation, in June 1940, he enlisted in the RCAF where he served as a bomber pilot. In October 1941 he was taken prisoner on a

Author with wife Wynne and daughter Candace at the RCAF ex-POW reunion in Ottawa, 1989.

mission over Germany. His story for the next three and one half years is chronicled herein. He was liberated in April, 1945, and shortly thereafter married Wynne Moores, the young WAAF from London, England whose letters had sustained him through his internment in Germany.

After returning to Canada, Mr. Woolley worked for Imperial Oil in Toronto until his retirement in 1983. He and Wynne have two daughters, and three grandchildren to date. He obtained his Certified Management Accountant designation in

1971, and is presently taking university credit courses in Arts at Carleton University in Ottawa.

Air Force POW reunions take place every three or four years and have been hosted in England, Australia, Canada and the U.S. Ted and Wynne have travelled to England for past reunions and look forward to a reunion there again in 1991. The close relationships established during the war years have been maintained by these regular POW gatherings, and as time passes and their numbers diminish, says Ted, the bonds grow ever stronger.